# From Law to Logos

# From Law to Logos

*Reading St. Paul's Epistle to the Galatians*

Jon R. Jordan

FOREWORD BY
Todd D. Still

WIPF & STOCK · Eugene, Oregon

FROM LAW TO LOGOS
Reading St. Paul's Epistle to the Galatians

Wipf & Stock
An Imprint of Wipf and Stock Publishers
199 W. 8th Ave., Suite 3
Eugene, OR 97401

www.wipfandstock.com

PAPERBACK ISBN: 978-1-4982-8970-2
HARDCOVER ISBN: 978-1-4982-8972-6
EBOOK ISBN: 978-1-4982-8971-9

Manufactured in the U.S.A.

For my children,
who can't yet read Galatians,
but are even now receiving
grace and peace from their true Father.

# Contents

# Foreword

IF YOU ARE SEARCHING for a technical, scholarly treatment of Galatians from a New Testament specialist, then *From Law to Logos* is not for you. You may go ahead and put this book down. If, however, you are interested in becoming a student of Scripture and in reading Galatians with the guidance of a well-informed, insightful Christian with seminary training, then *From Law to Logos* just may well be your cup of tea.

In this valuable, accessible volume, Jon R. Jordan displays his considerable skill as a pedagogue as he guides readers through Paul's sometimes surprising, frequently demanding, always engaging Letter to the Galatians. After orienting readers to ancient letters in general and to Galatians in particular, Jordan examines Paul's impassioned, pastoral missive section by section. In so doing, Jordan enables his audience to think the Apostle's thoughts after him.

In a day when interest in and knowledge of Scripture are not as great as one might wish, Jordan's slender, sympathetic study serves as a welcomed entrée to Galatians. What is more, his invitation to read the letter again and again and to be open to the transformative power of the gospel declared therein is as refreshing as it is timely.

Todd D. Still
DeLancey Dean and Hinson Professor
Baylor University, Truett Seminary
Waco, Texas

# Preface

THE MORE I TEACH and interact with Christians from across a broad spectrum of ages, the more I am convinced that something odd happens to otherwise-intelligent readers when they sit down to read the Bible. Want to see what I am talking about for yourself? In the middle of the Fall, try asking someone who enjoys football what they think about the next big match-up. Sit and listen as they—from memory—regurgitate the injury report for each team, the relative offensive and defensive rankings, and even the weather forecast and its potential impact on the game. It turns out that most of us know how to read, can retain large amounts of information, and are able to research the mess out of things we truly enjoy. But when we sit down to read the Bible, something changes. We suddenly feel out of our element. Sentences stop making sense, and we quickly lose confidence in our ability to understand the meaning of what we are reading.

There are many reasons for this. Some of them are not our fault, but others certainly are. On the not-quite-our-fault end of the spectrum is the basic reality that the Bible is a collection of ancient documents written in languages that are unfamiliar to most of its readers. It also contains countless cultural references and illustrations that seem puzzling to 21st century westerners. The Bible, compared to other literature, is by its very nature difficult to read. But with a few trustworthy guides, the modern reader can overcome many of the difficulties that arise from the fact that the Bible is a collection of ancient Near Eastern texts written thousands of years ago. Part of the reason I wrote this book was to take some of the edge off of this difficulty for readers of Galatians.

The Bible is also difficult to read because of the unfair expectations we often impose on it. We cannot help but read the Bible in light of our current life situations. This is part of what it means to be a human reader of a text.[1] We can, however, avoid using this reality to place unfair expectations on the text we are reading. How do we place unfair expectations on the Bible? We turn to it in search of specific answers to specific questions we happen to have in a given moment, and are disappointed when it fails to deliver nuggets of wisdom after we have spent only a few minutes searching for them.

Imagine that you are struggling with a difficult decision. You open your Bible hoping to gain some wisdom, and you turn to Psalm 137. This imprecatory Psalm has nothing to do with decision-making, so you close your Bible in frustration. Or maybe you are a bit more tenacious, and turn to several more passages in search of direction. Even if you spent a significant amount of time searching, the chances of finding a passage that speaks directly to your situation are minimal.[2] This is simply not how the Bible is meant to be read.

The Bible becomes more difficult to understand, and less relevant to our lives, when we demand direct application that matches our exact situation at the moment we are reading the text. The Bible's purpose is less about providing quotable advice for our current situations, and more about painting a grand vision of ultimate reality that is centered around the death and resurrection of

1. There are some approaches to reading the Bible that ask the reader to come to the text without their own preconceived notions in mind. This "blank slate" approach is simply not possible. We *will* bring our own perceptions of God and the World to the Bible. Our best hope is to do all that we can to bring better preconceptions to the text; something the early Church called reading with the "rule of faith" in mind.

2. Even those passages that include significant decision-making techniques (Gideon's Fleece in Judges 6 and the Apostles' casting of lots in Acts 1, for example) have never been understood to be instructive on how to make decisions, but merely descriptive of how decisions were made by some people throughout God's history of interacting with humanity.

the Son of God. This grand vision certainly has an impact on our current situation, but we should not expect direct, personal advice from a book that is primarily about God and His purposes, not humans and our purposes.

I hope that as you spend time with this book, and, more importantly, with St. Paul's epistle to the Galatians, you will see this grand vision of ultimate reality more clearly. In doing so, as Christians have done throughout the centuries, I think you will find that seeing yourself and your situation within this grand vision will ultimately be more helpful to you than any bit of advice you originally thought you needed.

Reading the Bible is not an easy task. I hope that this book will be one of many guides that help you overcome the hurdles we face when approaching our sacred text.

Jon R. Jordan
*Feast of St. Peter & St. Paul*
June 2016

# Acknowledgments

These chapters are, in large part, the result of a Young Adults Bible Study I was invited to teach at Church of the Incarnation in Dallas, TX. I would like to thank Ryan Waller and the Incarnation Foundation for the opportunity to spend time teaching through Galatians with a group of bright, curious, and eager parishioners.

Several students and friends provided helpful feedback on early drafts of this book. I would like to especially thank Aaron, Clark, Charles, Jacob, Jenni, and Tyson. This book makes more sense because of them.

It would be an extreme oversight on my part if I did not thank my wife, Vivien, for the sacrifices she made to create time for me to work on this book, and for her tireless encouragement all along the way.

# 1

# How to Read this Book

## A Book About a Book

THIS IS A BOOK about a book. Depending on who you are, that is either exciting news or the first sign that you should close this book and never open it again. I hope that you continue, because there are certain books that are really worth reading, and this book is about one of those books.[1]

We live in a world that is shaped by significant texts. From Plato's *Republic* to the *Magna Carta* to *Harry Potter*, much of how we view the world is informed by the written word. The Christian Scriptures—the Hebrew Bible and the New Testament—are must-reads for any Christian that is seriously seeking to live out their baptismal calling in the context of the local church and the wider world.

There are times to read the Scriptures as inspirational pick-me-ups, and there are times to spend countless hours pulling our hair out in frustration over what these texts actually mean. In either case, God's people are well served to carefully consider the text they are reading and its implications for our life together.

These texts that we call Scripture were written in a different language than our own, in a different region of the world than our

1. If you decide to keep reading—and I do hope you will—please stop and read the Preface if you haven't already.

own, and from a cultural and philosophical perspective that few of us share today. Simply put: any collection of ancient texts is difficult for modern readers to translate and understand. The Bible is no exception to this rule. And Galatians, one of the most explored texts throughout Christian history, is also no exception.

But do we really need a book about how to read it?

We do. In fact, we need a lot of books about how to read St. Paul's epistle to the Galatians, and fortunately, we *do* have a lot of books to read about Galatians. There are countless commentaries on Galatians, each with their own unique contribution to our understanding of the epitsle. Galatians continues to captivate the imagination of biblical scholars, who hold conferences and write books and contribute to academic journals in order to further unpack the meaning of Galatians and its implications for the church today.

Unless you have spent time in seminary or have done graduate work in other fields, it may be surprising that there are countless scholars alive today who have spent their lives interacting with Galatians. It might even seem like a bit much. Can't we all just read the Bible for ourselves? Wasn't this the point of the Reformation? What gives someone else the right to tell me how to interpret the Bible?

To those who are skeptical about the need for biblical scholarship—those who just want Jesus and their Bible and to be left well enough alone—I would ask this: how is that working for you? How confident are you in your own interpretation of the text? When you read a passage of Scripture and a potential interpretation emerges in your imagination, why do you trust that interpretation? In what other areas of life do your initial gut reactions turn out to be the best reactions? How well does the "what this verse means to me" approach to studying the Bible fit within the Bible's command to take every thought captive? What do you do when other well-meaning, Bible-believing Christians arrive at different conclusions than you?

The goal in asking these questions is not to convince readers to become biblical scholars or to go to seminary. For a vast majority of Christians working in or studying for careers in other industries, neither of these are realistic possibilities. The goal is to bring to mind the necessity for *help* in reading the Scriptures, and the futility of trying to be theological Lone Rangers. There have been wise interpreters of Scripture throughout history and today who have spent more time in study and prayer than we have, and it is worth listening to what they have to say about Galatians.

One goal of this book is to summarize what some of these thinkers have had to say about Galatians. But that is not the only goal of this book. Scholars have much to offer us as we seek to understand Scripture, but it is important to remember that Galatians was not written to be studied in an academic setting. It was written for people like you and me.

Galatians was written for people who sometimes find themselves swinging back and forth between trying to be good enough for God and trying not to be as bad as we know we are capable of being. Galatians was written for people who feel superior to others when their life is going as planned, and for people who are close to giving up on the faith because of how they are treated by fellow Christians who seem to hold others to impossibly high standards, while refusing to apply those same standards to their own life. Yes, Galatians was written *to* a specific group of regional churches in the middle of the first century, but Galatians was also written *for* people like you and me. And Galatians was meant to be read.

So this is the other goal of this book: to equip and encourage you to read Galatians over and over again for the rest of your life.

## Reading Galatians Again and Again

While on a trip to Europe with my wife in the summer of 2012, I attended a conference on Galatians at the University of St. Andrews. To begin the conference, the attendees were taken on a walking tour of the town. We walked past the famous golf course, and toured some of the oldest buildings on campus. At the end of the tour, we were all corralled into a room that seemed just a bit too small for a group of roughly one hundred of us. Once we were all standing in the room — and I do mean standing — one of the doctoral students was instructed to read Galatians aloud.

The next half-hour or so was spent listening to St. Paul's first-century pastoral epistle to the Galatian churches. As we listened, I became increasingly aware that I stood in a long line of Christians who have heard Galatians read aloud. I felt, perhaps for the first time in my life, that I was *receiving* the Word of God. I was not discovering it on my own, and I was not mining it for information or answers to my ethical dilemmas. I was simply listening to two-thousand-year-old words written to someone else that somehow seemed to be speaking directly to me.

I will most likely never return to that room, and because of how surprised I was by the experience itself, I will likely never be able to recreate what I felt that day. But the environment of that specific room with those specific people was only part of what made the moment so special for me. This was also the first time I heard Galatians in a single setting. As much as I had studied Galatians, and had even been required to translate portions of it from its original language in the classroom, I had never read it in its entirety all at once. Your experience may be different than mine here —and hopefully it is — but I had never really considered that I *should* read Galatians all at once, the way I would read any other letter.

As you read this book, I will ask you to take time to also read the entire text of Galatians itself as often as you can. This book is designed to introduce you to major literary, historical, and theological themes that you will encounter in each section of Galatians. As you spend time studying the individual pieces of the Galatian puzzle, don't forget to spend even more time soaking up the image the whole puzzle creates. At the end of each chapter you will find a section, entitled *This Time Through Galatians*, that asks you to read Galatians again, giving special attention to the new information you just learned.

## This Time Through Galatians

Even before we get into How to Read an Epistle (chapter 2) and Introduction to Galatians (chapter 3), spend some time reading Galatians all the way through. Whether this is your first time reading the letter in its entirety or you have spent serious time studying this text, try to hear Paul's deep concern for the Galatian churches. If at all possible, find someone to read with you. If you are studying as part of a group, spend some time during your first gathering reading the letter aloud.

My recommendation is that you annotate the same copy of Galatians each time you read it. I have included the full text of the New English Translation of Galatians as an appendix. Depending on your preference, you might want to print a copy of your favorite translation to keep folded inside this book, or you might want to simply annotate the Bible you most regularly use. Either way I think that you will find that annotating Galatians while you discover more and more about its context throughout this book will be a helpful exercise in becoming increasingly familiar with this ancient epistle. If you are really into annotating texts as you read them—and I think you should be—then you might want to consider using a different color pen or pencil for each time you read Galatians after finishing a chapter in this book.

# 2

# How to Read an Epistle

## Epistles in the New Testament

LETTERS ARE FASCINATING TO read, especially when you recognize that they are letters and treat them as such. Imagine finding a hand-written letter in your attic written from your dad to your mom on the day they found out that they were expecting you. Reading this letter has the potential to be a very special moment in your life, an opportunity to look back in time at the love shared between your parents before you took all of their free time and sanity away from them.

> Dear Love of Mine,
>
> I can not begin to tell you how amazing you looked this morning as you shared the big news with me. Today is the beginning of a new phase in our life together. I love you, I will always love you, and I love the child growing inside of you even now.
>
> Yours until death do us part,
>
> Dave

What would happen if you were a lazy reader who failed to take the genre of the document you are holding into account? Or what if you knew that you were reading a letter, but you didn't take the time to discover who wrote it, to whom it was addressed, when it was originally written, or what context surrounded its writing? And perhaps most awkwardly of all scenarios, what if you read a sentence or two from the middle of the letter and assumed that it was meant specifically for you? In other words, how strange would it be for you to read this attic letter the same way that, unfortunately, many of us read the Bible?

It is lazy and irresponsible to ignore genre when reading any piece of literature, especially literature that is labeled Scripture.

I hope that last line worries us all a bit. Are we putting our God-given ability to think and reason to use as we read the Bible? Although a little bit of intimidation is appropriate when approaching a sacred text, we should not let this fear cripple our desire to continue reading the Bible. You do not need to understand the deep intricacies of ancient Near Eastern literary genre to learn from our Scriptures. But a basic understanding of the prominent genres of the New Testament and the specific text you are reading will, I think, prove quite valuable as you seek to encounter God in the Scriptures.

Galatians is an epistle—a letter sent to a person or group of people— written by St. Paul and some fellow Christians to various churches in the region of Galatia (modern-day Turkey). If you want to read the New Testament well, you need to learn how to read epistles. Of the 27 books of the New Testament, 21 are epistles. Even the Book of Revelation, which is technically apocalyptic literature and is not included among the 21 epistles of the New Testament, contains seven small epistles within its opening chapters. Understanding the genre of epistle is clearly important for understanding the New Testament.

If you have spent time studying literature from different eras it will be no surprise to you that the form and style of epistles have varied throughout history and among different cultures. In the world that the authors of New Testament epistles inhabited, there were several popular types of letters. Two primary types of letters— those written by Greeks in the Greek-speaking world and those written by Hebrews living in the Greek-speaking world—appear to serve as models for most of the epistles of the New Testament. When thinking about the culture and ethnicity of the authors and original audiences of the texts that make up the New Testament, it should come as no surprise that these types of letters—Greek and Hebrew—would be used as models for most New Testament epistles.

As readers of epistles, it is also important to learn as much as we can about the context of a given letter before reading it. There are four key components of a New Testament epistle that are crucial to understand when it comes to interpreting and applying these letters as Scripture. Before you read a New Testament epistle, discover as much as you can about (1) the author, (2) the audience, (3) the occasion, and (4) the purpose of the letter. The rest of this chapter explains the significance of each of these four components, and gives hints about how to discover them before you read. The next chapter will explore the author, audience, occasion, and purpose of Galatians itself.

A quick note is in order regarding spoilers when reading any written work. If you are one who tends to enjoy surprises, and cannot stand it when people ruin endings for you, maybe consider reading a New Testament epistle once-through before actually sitting down to study it. Studying the author, audience, occasion, and purpose will give away a good amount of any suspense you may find throughout an epistle. But once you have read it all the way through and are now ready to begin studying it, your mind needs to shift from entertainment-mode to learning-mode. Eventually you will find that learning mode is actually quite pleasurable, but at first I would not be surprised if you find that it takes considerable effort to sit down and re-read an epistle dozens of times in order to continue learning what it is trying to teach.

It may be worth thinking more about these two ways of approaching reading: reading for entertainment and reading for learning. Imagine watching the television series LOST. The first time that you watch the series, your primary concern is likely related to the mysterious elements of the plot and setting; you are watching for entertainment. You faced a week of agony between each episode—something that those of us who watched it before Netflix was around were forced to endure—because you had questions that needed answers, and you were convinced that the next episode would provide those very answers. This cliff-hanging experience only increased the entertainment value. But now imagine that after you have seen the entire series, you decide to re-watch LOST in order to explore what you may have missed when your primary concern was jumping from one cliff-hanger to another in search of answers to your ever-increasing plot-based questions. This second time through you might notice the series' use of the colors white and black, the curiously large number of characters named after prominent philosophers, and the subtle ways that elements of the plane crash in the pilot episode foreshadowed much of the island conflict. When we shift from entertainment-mode to learning-mode, our approach may change but it does not mean that our reading experience will be any less exciting.

With this in mind, and with our learning-mode mindset fully enabled, let's move on to the first two components to explore when studying an epistle: the author and the audience.

## Author and Audience

The form of a letter—how it was structured and the type of language it used—told ancient audiences what to expect from the letter. This still happens today. If you were to discover a letter in your mailbox addressed to "Current Resident," you already know that this letter is likely an advertisement of some sort. If you were to find an envelope with handwritten letters addressed to "Our Grandson," you would know immediately that unless the local cable company has developed brilliant customer acquisition techniques, the letter in your hands is personal and from someone that cares about you. How a letter is addressed actually has an impact on our interpretation of that letter, often before we even read the contents of the letter itself.

Modern letters tend to begin by listing the audience of the letter first: "Dear Frank," "To Whom it May Concern," etc. We have been trained to discover the audience of a letter by reading the salutation, which is most frequently found in the opening words of the letter. Ancient letters, especially those letters whose style New Testament authors tend to use, are different. They begin not by naming the audience, but by naming the author or authors.

Not only do authors of New Testament epistles generally begin by listing their name first, they also often expand upon their name in a way that serves their purpose for writing. Depending on what the author intends to communicate they may highlight one or more aspects of their lives in the opening of their letters. At times, for example, Paul introduces himself as an apostle, while at other times he introduces himself as a servant. In the next chapter we will see how Paul actually begins part of his argument in the way he introduces himself in his letter to the Galatians.

This is all hopefully some interesting background information, but you probably already knew that Paul wrote Galatians. Why does it matter that Paul and other New Testament authors often followed pre-existing epistle forms? There are several advantages to knowing this information, but let's think about two of them. First, when New Testament authors *deviate* from common forms of their day, there might be significance to that deviation. If, for example, it was common to open an epistle with a lengthy greeting, but an author chooses to jump immediately into the content of the letter they may be communicating a sense of urgency. This is lost on the modern reader if they know nothing about the genre of ancient epistles.

The second advantage of knowing about ancient epistles has less to do with interpreting them and more to do with how we should interact in our own time and culture. In learning about ancient genres a simple but significant reality is brought to our attention: authors of biblical texts used genres and styles common to their day in order to communicate the radical news of what God had done through Jesus Christ. In addition to helping us understand the letters themselves, this reality also gives us permission to do the same. As much as I am personally a fan of books as means of communication, I am also excited to know that there are

Christians on the frontiers of new media, exploring new ways of sharing a very old story.

## Occasion and Purpose

In addition to learning as much as you can about the author and audience of an epistle, there are two important things to explore before diving in: the occasion and the purpose. These two are certainly linked to one another, but are distinct enough to spend time considering them each individually.

The occasion of a letter refers to the circumstances that caused to the author to write the letter. In one moment, Paul is not writing Galatians, and in the next moment he is. The occasion of a letter answers the question *what sparked the author's writing of the letter*?

The purpose answers a different, though related question: *what point is the author trying to make in this letter*? Given the occasion of the letter, what is the author arguing for or against?

Knowing the occasion of an epistle is an important step in understanding its purpose, but it does not automatically tell you its purpose. Imagine that you are in a long-term dating relationship, and you receive a text message that simply reads "Sorry, but I think we should break up. It's not you, it's me." After recovering from your initial devastation, you sit down to write a letter to your not-so-significant-anymore other. Receiving the initial text message would be considered the *occasion* of your letter, the event that sparked the writing of your own letter. But at this point there are still a number of options on the table for the *purpose* of your letter. If you sit down to write a lengthy "I know I was wrong and I promise to be better" letter, then your purpose is to convince the reader to give you a second chance. If instead you write a brief "here is a list of everything I never liked about you" letter, then your purpose is to convince the reader that you are not even that sad about the breakup, and that you will be just fine without them. (Whether this is true or not will remain your secret).

If someone only had access to your letter, and knew nothing about the text message that sparked the writing of the letter, it would be more difficult to properly interpret the letter. The "list of everything wrong with you" letter, for example, might appear to be its own (rather harsh) breakup letter. Generations of interpreters would be operating under the false assumption that the author of your letter initiated the break-up. While this assumption would not negatively affect *every* aspect of the letter's interpretation, it would certainly fall short of the best understanding of the letter's original purpose.

The occasion of a letter helps us better understand the purpose of the letter. Understanding both the occasion and the purpose of an epistle makes us better readers and interpreters.

## This Time Through Galatians

Sometimes it is necessary to go beyond an epistle itself to discover important information about its author, audience, occasion, and purpose. This is certainly true for Galatians, as you will find in the next chapter.

That being said, there is much to discover about these aspects of the epistle within the text of Galatians itself. As you pause to read through Galatians this time, look for and annotate things you discover about the author, audience, occasion, and purpose of Paul's epistle to the Galatians.

# 3

# Introduction to Galatians

I HOPE THAT BY now you agree that in order to better read and interpret a New Testament epistle you must learn something about its author, audience, occasion, and purpose. What follows in this chapter is a brief introduction to Galatians that does just that.

## The Author

St. Paul has captured the imagination of every generation of Christian thinkers from his own day to ours. This is the type of thing that happens to you when you write most of the New Testament. For the reader of Galatians, it is helpful to know the author of Galatians as his audience knew him. We can gather a good deal of information about Paul from his letter to the Galatians itself. While most of our emphasis in this chapter will be on Galatians-specific things to know about Paul, a brief biographical sketch of the Apostle may be helpful first.

### Biographical Sketch

The man we know today as St. Paul the Apostle was actually born in the city of Tarsus in Cilicia and given the name Saul. He was a Hebrew, born into the tribe of Benjamin, and was raised as a Pharisee.

Before his conversion to Christianity, Paul joined in the active persecution of Christians. He was converted when Jesus himself appeared to him while on his way to persecute Christians in the city of Damascus. After his conversion, Paul began a series of extensive church planting missions across the Roman Empire. Many of his letters to these churches were quickly recognized as Scripture and made their way into the New Testament.[1]

It is worth spending some time understanding one crucial aspect of Paul's background that will prove important throughout his letter to the Galatians: his former life as a Pharisee. What did it mean to be a Pharisee in Paul's day?

## Paul, the Pharisee

Like most religions today, Judaism in the 1st century had a variety of (often competing) parties. Many of these sects operated similarly to the way Christian denominations do today. You have likely read about some of the more popular ones in the Gospels, possibly without recognizing them as distinct sects: the Sadducees, the Pharisees, and the Zealots.[2] Each of these groups were rooted in Jewish tradition and the Scriptures that we call the Old Testament. Understanding a bit about each of these sects will help us understand why Paul, a former Pharisee, is so equipped to write the epistle to the Galatians.

Unfortunately, relatively little is known about the Sadducees. None of their written works are available to us today, and they are not referenced as frequently as other major sects in the New Testament or in other ancient works. What we do know about them comes to us from the Gospels and a Jewish historian named Josephus, who himself happened to be a Pharisee. From both of these sources we learn that the Sadducees likely did not believe in the

1. Even as other New Testament texts were still being written, the writings of Paul were held in high regard. See 2 Peter 3:15–16.

2. The Essenes are another fascinating sect worthy of study. Little was known about them until the discovery of the Dead Sea Scrolls in the middle of the 20th century.

immortality of the soul or in the resurrection of the dead. Josephus also claims that they viewed God as more distant than did other Jewish sects, who tended to emphasize and hope for God's continual acting within human history. Many of the High Priests and other religious rulers in Paul's day identified as Sadducees, and it is made clear in multiple sources that they often had heated disputes with the Pharisees.

The Zealots, on the other hand, agreed in many areas with the Pharisees. As their name suggests, the primary difference between them and the Pharisees was their zeal that often came in the form of leading armed revolts against their oppressors. According to Josephus, they were not afraid to face death, and often were found at the center of armed conflicts with the Romans.

This brings us, finally, to the Pharisees. This sect of Judaism believed in the resurrection of the dead, and believed that God was active in the world. They were known for their piety, particularly in public. They longed for the day when God would return to His people and make things right. They knew the Old Testament Law—or Torah—and they sought to interpret it precisely and to challenge those who they believed were interpreting it incorrectly. A quick reading of the Gospels will highlight this aspect of Pharisaical thought. There were no higher first-century authorities when it came to interpreting and applying the Old Testament Law than the Pharisees.

Throughout his ministry of teaching and healing, Jesus had more than his fair share of disputes with the Pharisees. As we will discover in Galatians, this dispute between followers of Jesus and the Pharisees spilled into the earliest decades of the Christian Church. Galatians has at its center a dispute about the relationship between the Old Testament Law and the Christian faith. Who better to settle this dispute than a former Pharisee who through an encounter with Jesus was converted to Christianity and made an Apostle to the Gentile world?

## Paul in Galatians

We turn now to how Paul portrays himself throughout Galatians. In this epistle, he presents himself as (1) an apostle (2) who received a special revelation from the risen Jesus that caused him to leave his former life as a Pharisee and persecutor of the Christian Church in order to (3) plant a series of mostly Gentile Churches across the Roman empire. These three aspects of Paul's life will be explored below.

### *Paul, the Apostle*

If you did not know that Paul was an Apostle before reading Galatians, you certainly are left without an excuse after reading it. The first words of Galatians are "Paul, an apostle," and a majority of the opening chapter and a half are spent defending his status as an Apostle. Why? Paul had planted the Galatian Churches and was therefore already seen as an authority within those churches. Why does he feel the need to stress the fact that he is an Apostle?

From the very earliest days of the Church, special authority was placed on those who had been chosen to be Apostles. These Apostles primarily included the Twelve Disciples (minus Judas Iscariot). In the first chapter of Acts of the Apostles, the church fills the empty spot left by Judas with a man named Matthias. Later in Acts, we see the conversion of St. Paul, who would soon begin to be recognized as an Apostle as well. By writing to the Galatians as an Apostle, Paul is writing with the authority given to Him by Jesus himself. He is to be trusted more than other teachers, as we will hear him argue in the early chapters of Galatians, by virtue of his status as an Apostle.

As modern readers of Galatians—who already know the impact Paul had on the early Christian Church—it is easy to feel as though spending the opening chapters of this letter defending his status as an apostle is a bit of an overkill. Two important points are worth considering here: (1) Galatians is a very early (if not the earliest) Pauline letter, and (2) it mattered a great deal to the Galatians whether Paul—who was physically absent—was to be trusted more that other teachers who had moved in to the area while Paul was away.[3]

## Paul, the Radical Convert

Paul is very aware that his status as an Apostle is unique among the other Apostles.[4] The other Twelve had spent time with Jesus before his death and resurrection. They made up his inner-core of disciples, and they were present for many of his miracles and most notorious teachings. It was to them that Jesus gave the Great Commission in Matthew 28. It was these same disciples who were hiding in a room when Jesus appeared to them after His resurrection, and who were later seen boldly proclaiming the Good News of God in the Acts of the Apostles.

All the while a Pharisee named Saul of Tarsus was doing everything he could to destroy this new sect of Christians, this small but growing band of *little Christs*. His conversion was not slow and steady. The Bible describes him as still "breathing threats and murder against the disciples of the Lord" when Jesus appeared before him on the road to Damascus, leaving him blind.

Saul of Tarsus underwent a radical change because of his encounter with Jesus, and emerged as Paul, the Apostle. His experience as a Pharisee, his radical conversion, and the direct revelation he received from the risen Jesus are all used throughout Galatians to bolster his argument.

As we can see throughout his letters, Paul fully embraced the risen Jesus as the Messiah. He was, in this sense, explicitly Christian. This does not mean, however, that he abandoned all that he once knew as a Pharisee. Paul remained committed to the God who was revealed in the Scriptures of the Old Testament, and continued to insist on properly interpreting these Scriptures. In his

---

3. We will learn more about this group of teachers soon.

4. Most specifically seen in Galatians 1:1, 12, 15–17.

conversion, Paul did not abandon the revelation of God in the Old Testament and in the Law. Instead, as we see throughout Galatians, he reinterprets everything—including the Old Testament and the Law—in light of God's truest revelation to humanity: the person and work of Jesus Christ.

## Paul, the Apostle to the Gentiles.

A quick reading of Acts and the New Testament epistles will reveal that St. Paul was especially called to be an "apostle to the Gentiles."[5] After spending some time in relative silence, Paul begins an impressive series of Church planting missions, primarily in the Gentile world. Paul is credited with planting churches all the way from Syria to Greece, and he wrote to and visited even more geographically wide-spread churches such as the church in Rome. The Apostle Paul wrote Galatians to one such collection of Gentile Churches in the region of Galatia.

Given his extensive background in Judaism, you might think that he would be more suited to be an apostle to his own (Jewish) people.[6] As we will soon discover in Galatians—perhaps more so than in any other epistle—Paul's background in Judaism is in fact the very thing that makes his argument so powerful among a primarily Gentile audience.

## The Audience

Galatia—as opposed to Corinth or Ephesus—refers to a region, not a city. By default this makes the audience of Paul's letter more broad than other epistles he wrote, and it means that we actually know less about the specific audience than we would like to know. There is a fairly long-standing dispute among interpreters regarding the precise audience of Paul's letter. As odd as it may seem

---

5. See Galatians 2:8 and Ephesians 1:1, for example.

6. See summaries of Paul's life in Judaism in Galatians 1:13–14 and Philippians 3:4–6.

to those of us who have access to advanced GPS technology in our pockets, much of the debate centers around where Galatia was actually located. In case you happen to encounter these debates in Commentaries, a brief summary of the two leading contenders is provided below.[7]

The oldest view among interpreters is that Galatians was written to a group of churches in a country in Asia Minor called Galatia. This view is called the Northern Galatian theory since it would place the audience of Galatians primarily in the northern portion of modern-day Turkey. This view, based on the known missionary journeys of Paul, would mean that Galatians was written somewhere around AD55, much closer to the writing of Romans. This would still make Galatians one of Paul's earliest letters, but not by much. Another implication of this view is that Galatians would have been written after the crucial Jerusalem Council that is recorded in Acts 15. In this Council, the Church leaders in Jerusalem gave their official answer to the question about to what extent Gentile converts to Christianity were expected to follow the Old Testament Law. As we will soon discover, this is also one of the central concerns of the letter to the Galatians.

Other interpreters think "Galatia" refers to the Roman province of Galatia, which would include a much wider area of land, especially to the South of the traditional Northern view. Mustering all the creative energy they had left after studying ancient texts over the course of a lifetime, interpreters have generally referred to this position as the Southern Galatian theory. In addition to a different geographical location for the audience of Galatians, there are also a few important implications for the date of the letter. If the Southern theory is correct, then these Galatian churches were likely planted during Paul's earlier missionary journey beginning in Acts 11. This would place the letter of Galatians around AD50, if not earlier, and would make it Paul's earliest New Testament

7. In case you are thinking to yourself, "I don't think any of this actually matters." I would like to say two things. First, you are, to some extent, correct. But not entirely. Read on. Second, this summary is only a few paragraphs. We have all likely spent more time this week reading less important information.

epistle.[8] Galatians, then, would have been written before the Jerusalem Council took place, during a time when the question of Gentile observance of Jewish law was not quite settled.

While the thrust of the letter is able to be understood by modern readers regardless of which theory is correct, I hope that you see the importance of exploring questions like this. In the case of Galatians, a fascinating question is answered two different ways depending on which theory is accepted. Did Paul's argument in Galatians *flow out of the Jerusalem Council's decision*, or did it come before the Jerusalem Council and possibly *help shape that very decision*?

This historical question—and others like it—are worthy of being explored, and there are plenty of scholars currently doing just that. But it is also possible to be aware of and intrigued by questions like this without trying to answer them ourselves. It is usually best for those of us who are not professional academic theologians to simply move on from these debates and continue our discovery of what else Galatians has to say, and what it has to say to us. I include interpretive disagreements like this throughout this book because I have found, as I imagine you will as well, that knowing a little bit about these types of questions has caused my reading of Galatians to be more interesting and insightful than it would be without them. If nothing else, these questions remind me that I will never reach the bottom of the well of Galatians, or any other Biblical text. The basic messages of the various texts that make up the Christian Scriptures may be simple, but they are not shallow. They can be understood on one level by the youngest of readers, and yet they provide plenty of material for interpreters to explore throughout an entire lifetime.

---

8. It is entirely likely that Paul wrote countless other epistles that did not survive or were not preserved to the same extent as his New Testament epistles.

## The Occasion and Purpose

J. Louis Martyn once said that to read the letter of Galatians "is to be involved in high drama."[9] In Galatians we see a side of Paul that is seldom seen elsewhere in the New Testament. In a single letter he commends his audience's warm friendship, considers himself like a mother to them, and yet chastises them as "fools" for their abandonment of his message. And like a loving parent, he has even sharper words for those who are harming his children in the faith, not-so-subtly calling for them to be "cut off" in the context of a conversation about circumcision.[10] All this will be explored in later chapters, but it is shared here to make one simple point: something significant happened that caused Paul to sit down and write this passionate, dramatic letter.

After Paul had planted a series of Churches in Galatia and moved on to another region, a group of Jewish-Christian teachers moved into Galatia and began teaching the Gentile Christians that circumcision was necessary to truly belong to the people of God. After their message was presumably accepted by many within Galatia, word began to reach Paul, sparking the writing of his letter to the Galatians.

We know fewer details about these Teachers than we would like, but we can gather some information about them from the text of Galatians itself.[11] Paul specifically references them—though not by name—at least five times throughout the letter. According to Paul, these teachers were perverting the one true Gospel of Jesus (1:7), had bewitched the Galatian Christians who believed them (3:1), and had selfish motives for teaching what they taught (4:17, 6:12–13). It is easy to see why "agitators" is a common name for

---

9. Martyn, *Galatians*, 13.

10. Let that one sink in for a moment.

11. This group has been assigned several names throughout the history of interpreting Galatians. For our purposes we will simply refer to them as the Teachers.

this group of teachers in Commentaries throughout Christian History.[12]

Put simply, the occasion of Galatians is Paul hearing that a group of people had been teaching Gentile Christians in Galatia that they must be circumcised in order to fully belong to God's family. The purpose of the letter, then, is to convince the Galatians to abandon this new Gospel presented by these Teachers, and to return to the Gospel taught by Paul.

While it will be made clear as we dive further into Galatians itself, this is as good a place as any to point out something important about Paul's tone throughout this letter. For those of us who have never lived within Judaism, or who are not as entrenched in the Old Testament as we should be, the question of whether or not to be circumcised seems, on the surface, similar to other questions we see debated within the church today. Should I dress up when I go to church? Should we sing hymns or contemporary praise songs? Should a Christian be circumcised? Can a Christian get a tattoo?

Paul's tone throughout the letter is our first clue that Galatians is not Paul's position paper on an issue where there is room for disagreement among faithful Christians. Paul is not presenting his view on circumcision as one view among many reputable positions. Instead, he presents the gospel of the Teachers as a different gospel, one that requires a complete abandonment of the one true Gospel in order to be embraced (1:6).

When Paul converted to Christianity, he did so because he recognized the fundamental shift that occurred through the life, death, resurrection, and ascension of Jesus of Nazareth. Saul the Pharisee—so consumed with viewing obedience to the Torah as the primary marker of a right relationship between God and man—became Paul the Christian, who saw in Jesus both the end and the fulfillment of the Torah itself. This is why his reaction to the Teachers is so violent: Paul does not simply disagree with their

12. Paul uses the Greek words *tarassō* (to agitate/stir up) and *anastatoō* (to disturb, cause to rebel) throughout Galatians to describe these outside teachers.

interpretation of the ethical implications of the cross and resurrection. He sees their entire project of "Jesus plus Torah observance" as one that simply cannot exist now that Jesus has come.

For Paul, the Teachers are not simply wrong about one of the many details of the Christian faith. They are promoting a vision of reality that is completely incompatible with the vision of reality Paul himself received and preached as one of Christ's Apostles. This epistle was written to convince the Galatians to return again to the one true Gospel they received from Paul.

Now that we have a grasp of the author, audience, occasion, and purpose of Galatians, let's take a look at the overall structure of the epistle.

## Structure of the Argument

We have all found ourselves getting flustered when arguing about things that are very important to us. More often than not, our passion gets in the way of presenting a clear, sustained argument.[13] Fortunately for readers of Galatians, this is not the case for Paul. A quick reading of the epistle will reveal Paul's passion for the Galatians and the Gospel, but it will also reveal a well-organized and convincing argument.

If you ask a dozen scholars to provide an outline for Paul's epistle to the Galatians you will be presented with no less than thirteen possible options. That being said, most of those outlines will be variants of one basic outline, which we will adopt below.

The advantage of reading Galatians, in its entirety, over and over again is that you begin to make sense of individual verses in light of the overall structure of the letter. I think you will find the following approach to the structure of Galatians very helpful, especially once we begin exploring individual passages in greater detail. As always, it is good to keep in mind that outlines—like chapter and verse numbers—are meant to be helpful guides, but

13. See, for example, the internet.

it is always possible for them to get in the way of the meaning of the text.

Paul's argument throughout Galatians can generally be divided into three sections:

1. Paul's autobiographical defense of his credentials (1:1—2:14)

2. Paul's Theological Argument for his understanding of the Gospel (2:15—5:1)

3. The Practical Implications of Paul's understanding of the Gospel for the life of the Christian church (5:1—6:18)

Or, if we put these sections in the form of questions that we should expect to be answered:

1. Why should we trust Paul? (1:1—2:14)

2. What is Paul's Gospel? (2:15—5:1)

3. What changes in our individual and communal lives if Paul is right? (5:1—6:18)

It is helpful to know what to expect from each section, and to keep each section's purpose in mind as we seek to interpret individual passages in light of the entire epistle.


## This Time Through Galatians

As you read Galatians this time, note Paul's tone and sense of urgency throughout the letter. Let this time through Galatians serve as a reminder that Paul—and other authors of New Testament epistles—were writing primarily as concerned pastors. This does not mean that they were not theologians; the depths of their theological vision will not be exhausted this side of eternity. But it is always important to see how much of their writing is sparked by pastoral concern for actual people living in confusing and difficult times.

# 4

# Galatians and the Old Testament

FROM THE EARLIEST DAYS of the Christian Church, the collection of writings known as the Old Testament were viewed as part of the Christian Scriptures. New Testament authors relied heavily upon the Old Testament. The Old Testament is frequently quoted, alluded to, or otherwise referenced throughout the New Testament and by Jesus himself in the Gospels. Therefore, a basic understanding of the Old Testament is crucial for understanding most of the New Testament.

For readers of Galatians, there is a heightened need for understanding several aspects of the Old Testament. While not a sufficient summary of the Old Testament, what follows is a brief overview of some of its key events and people that will help you in your reading of Galatians.

This chapter presents a Christian reading of the Old Testament—one that reads much of what God revealed in and through Jesus back into the Old Testament. This way of reading the Old Testament is, as we will see, modeled by Paul himself throughout the New Testament and in Galatians. We also see Jesus read himself into the Old Testament in his conversation with the disciples on the road to Emmaus in Luke 24.

Given the occasion of the letter, much of what Paul will reference from the Old Testament will have to do with the Law and its relationship to God's people. In order to get our bearings before continuing to study Galatians, it will be helpful to paint a broad overview of the story of the Law in the Old Testament in three stages: (1) from Creation to Abraham, (2) from Abraham to the giving of the Law, and finally (3) the Law itself.[1]

## Creation to Abraham

The Hebrew people were convinced that "in the beginning" God created everything that exists. The earliest Christians reaffirmed this conviction, even as they sought to understand it in light of what God revealed in the life, death, and resurrection of Jesus. This led to an understanding that Jesus himself—before he "became flesh and dwelt among us"—was the instrument through which the world came into being. As Paul writes in Colossians 1, Jesus created all things, visible and invisible—both the elements of the universe and the "laws" that govern those elements. This notion will directly and indirectly play into Paul's argument about the Law throughout Galatians.

God created the world, looked out over his creation, and declared it "very good." Anyone familiar with the rest of Scripture knows that things do not remain very good for long. While the origin of evil is not addressed as clearly as we might like, what we do know from the Old Testament is that humanity gave into the temptation to be masters of their own lives—to live according to their own desires and not the desires of the God who made them. Special attention is given to the rebellion of Adam and Eve in Genesis 3, and much of the rest of the opening chapters of Genesis are an exposition of the extent of this rebellion. Genesis 1–11 recounts the earliest act of the great drama of human history: God created humanity, humanity rebelled, and they rebelled completely.

---

1. These somewhat artificial divisions are helpful for the purposes of studying Galatians, but are not necessarily the best at capturing the story and message of the Old Testament in its entirety.

## Abraham to the Law

In Genesis 12 we meet Abram, who through his encounter with God will come to be called Abraham.[2] It is through the life of Abraham that we begin to see more clearly the plan of God to restore humanity. Readers of Genesis quickly discover that it is through a covenant made with Abraham and his descendants that God will ultimately accomplish this restoration.

What is often lost when we read the story of Abraham is the reality that, from Abraham's perspective, God appeared to him out of the blue. When Abraham comes on the scene the only thing we know about him is that he was from the city-state of Ur, which by all accounts meant that he was involved in the worship of many gods. There was no Old Testament for him to read, there were no prophets of God for him to consult, and he did not belong to a community of people who regularly heard from God. He was, in this sense, alone. When God told Abraham and his family to pack their belongings and move to a new land, Abraham had no previous encounter with God to rely upon. Both Judaism and Christianity, for this reason, have always upheld Abraham as a supreme model of faith.

Throughout Abraham's lifetime, God made a series of promises to him. These promises have become known as the Abrahamic Covenant. God promised Abraham that he would have a son, and that through his son he would become the father of a great people, and that through that great people God would ultimately bless the entire world. Much of the rest of Genesis recounts how God's promise to Abraham was passed down from generation to generation. Abraham passed it on to his son Isaac, who passed it on to his son Jacob. After God renamed Jacob to Israel, the promise was passed down to Israel's sons, who would eventually become the namesakes of the Twelve Tribes of Israel. By the end of Genesis, the tribes of Israel had grown into a large community living in Egypt thanks to God's preservation through the life of Joseph.

---

2. Yes, that Abraham. As in "Father Abraham had many sons . . . "

As the reader of the Old Testament turns the page from the end of Genesis to the beginning of Exodus, they see that things began to take a turn for the worse. After the death of the Pharaoh who invited them to live in Egypt, the people of Israel were oppressed and eventually became slaves in the land. After centuries of slavery, God worked through the life of Moses to free his people from the oppression of the Egyptians, and lead them across the Red Sea to the base of Mount Sinai. It is at Sinai, centuries after the Covenant was given to Abraham, that God delivered the Law to his people through Moses.

## The Law

When the word Law is used in Scripture, it refers to more than just a list of instructions. The Hebrew word *Torah*, translated as Law throughout the Bible, refers to not just the 10 Commandments and the other laws that follow them, but also the entire narrative of the first five books of the Old Testament, commonly called the Pentateuch. The Law is not just the commandments given to Moses, it is God's revelation of his commands for Israel wrapped up in the story of Israel.

While the Law was more than just a list of rules, it was certainly not less than a list of rules. Chief among these rules are the 10 Commandments, listed in Exodus 20 and then again in Exodus 34. This collection of laws is among the most widely-recognized pieces of literature in Western civilization, and it still serves as Morality 101 for several world religions today. Much of the rest of the Pentateuch contains additional laws—as well as clarifications on existing laws—meant to govern Israel throughout the Old Testament.

Though they certainly rebelled against the Law at times, Israel held God's Law in high regard. The longest chapter in the Old Testament, Psalm 119, is a sustained meditation on the beauty and significance of God's Law. Towards the end of the Old Testament, a written copy of the Law was lost. Once it was rediscovered, the people of Israel reacted with a profound reverence as the Law was read aloud in its entirety.[3]

Far from a detached and obscure moral code, the Law was viewed by Israel as gracious revelation from God about how he designed human life to function.

While there have always been tendencies to diminish the importance of the Law throughout Christian history, Paul would not be counted among those who saw the Law as something to be ignored. He will certainly argue that the Law's purpose has already been fulfilled, but he will not diminish the significance of the Law itself.


## A Note on Circumcision

One aspect of the Law receives special attention in Paul's letter to the Galatians: circumcision.

While regulations regarding circumcision were included in the Law delivered to Moses at Sinai, the practice was actually first instituted during the life of Abraham, centuries before Moses and the giving of the Law:

> You shall be circumcised in the flesh of your foreskins, and it shall be a sign of the covenant between me and you. He who is eight days old among you shall be circumcised. Every male throughout your generations, whether born in your house or bought with your money from any foreigner who is not of your offspring, both he who is born in your house and he who is bought with your money, shall surely be circumcised. So shall my covenant be in your flesh an everlasting covenant. Any uncircumcised male who is not circumcised in the flesh of his foreskin shall be cut off from his people; he has broken my covenant. (Genesis 17:11–14)

Circumcision was given by God as an "everlasting covenant" to Abraham and to all those who would follow him. According to Genesis 17, those who refused to be circumcised would be "cut

---

3. See 2 Kings 22–23 and Nehemiah 8.

off" from God's people, and have broken His covenant. Let that sink in for a moment.

This is a significant reality to grasp before diving head-first into Galatians: Paul's opponents in Galatians had been making the case that in order to be considered a part of God's family, the Galatians must be circumcised. We must recognize that, although Paul will argue that they are wrong, they have a convincing *biblical* case here. Before Galatians was written, the odds were stacked against Paul. The plainest reading of Genesis 17 suggests that circumcision is to be practiced by all males who wanted to be considered part of God's family.

We fail to see the potency of their argument when we dismiss the Galatian Teachers as simply advocating a gospel of salvation by works. It is easy to suggest that they were merely advocating for a "Jesus + circumcision" gospel, and that the answer is to adopt a "Jesus + nothing" gospel. While this is a popular approach to the book of Galatians, and while it does carry with it elements of truth, it does not take into account the seriousness of the claims made by the Teachers. Their claim that those who want to be in God's family must be circumcised came directly from the very Scriptures that Paul honored as such.

This brings us back to the conflict over circumcision in Galatians. To combat the Teachers, Paul does not simply quote Scripture; he does the work of a theologian. That is to say, he uses Scripture to explain things about God that both honor the meaning of the biblical witness and that go beyond what any of the biblical texts say individually.

By the end of the epistle to the Galatians, the reader is left at a crossroads of sorts. Either Paul's understanding of Jesus and the Old Testament is correct, or the Galatian Teachers' understanding of Jesus and the Old Testament is correct. There is no room for both of them.

## This Time Through Galatians

As you read Galatians this time, make special note of every Old Testament reference you find. If you are familiar with the Old Testament person, concept, or event referenced by Paul, mark it with a star. If there are some Old Testament people, concepts, or events that you are not familiar with, circle them. As this book continues, you will hopefully find that many of the words you circle will be explained in later chapters, but you might also need to do some individual research while you continue to read Galatians.

# 5

# Why You Can Trust Paul:
# Galatians 1:1—2:14

PAUL'S PURPOSE IN THIS epistle is to convince the Galatian Christians that the Gospel he presented to them is the one true Gospel. Before entering in to a theological defense of his gospel, he spends the opening chapter and a half defending his own status as an Apostle. His purpose throughout Galatians 1:1—2:14 is to convince the Galatians that he is to be trusted more than the Teachers. Let's take a look at some of the key features of this section of Galatians.

## Dear Galatians: 1:1-5

Paul's greetings throughout the New Testament generally tend to follow common epistle greetings found elsewhere in the ancient world. These greetings can be broken into the following sections:

1. Naming of the author

2. Naming of the audience

3. Formal greeting

After the greeting, the rest of the epistle would contain the primary message, argument, or pronouncement of the letter itself. The epistle to the Galatians is no exception to this general pattern, but there are a few interesting deviations from Paul's own standard greeting found throughout the rest of his New Testament epistles that are worth noting here. These deviations occur in the naming of the author and formal greeting sections of Galatians. As you have likely noticed already, the naming of the audience in Galatians is a very straightforward "to the churches of Galatia," and there is little more to be said about this other than the Southern/Northern Galatia debate outlined in chapter 3. We will turn our attention now to the naming of the author and formal greeting sections.

## The Naming of the Author

Paul does not always list himself as the sole author of his epistles. In his letter to the Philippians, for example, Paul tells us in the opening verse that he and Timothy are the authors of the letter. Here in Galatians we notice by verse two that Paul is writing this letter along with "those who are with" him. He does not name these people, but it is safe to assume that it is important for Paul to inform the Galatians that he is not alone in his understanding of the Gospel. This letter is certainly from Paul, but it is also being sent with the support of those who are with him at the time of its writing.

The author of an epistle would often use various titles to describe themselves within their epistle's greeting. The titles they used to describe themselves often depended upon the content and purpose of the letter itself. Paul introduces himself in a variety of ways throughout the New Testament. In Romans, he introduces himself as "a slave of Jesus Christ" who was "called to be an apostle." In both Corinthians he introduces himself simply as "an apostle," while in Philippians he introduces himself simply as "a slave of Christ Jesus."

In Galatians, Paul introduces himself as "an apostle," but before moving on to naming his intended audience, he actually gives the reader a preview of the argument he plans to present throughout the first section of the letter. In other words, Paul begins defending his status as an apostle even before he finishes the first part of his greeting. This does not happen in any other New Testament epistle. Even from the introduction to his epistle it is clear to the reader that one of Paul's concerns is convincing the Galatians that he is an authority when it comes to the Gospel.

## Paul and his very long sentences

Even from the very beginning of Galatians the reader is introduced to one of Paul's most recognizable characteristics: he writes very long sentences. Now is a great time to discover how to make sense of them.

If you ever get bogged-down trying to make sense of Paul's long sentences, try to take a step back and see if you can find out which words make up his main point, and what words appear to be side notes or parenthetical expressions. All of these words matter, but it can be helpful to temporarily separate them from time to time. Let's try this with Paul's greeting in 1:1–2.

> Paul, an apostle—sent not by a group of people, nor by any individual person, but by Jesus Christ and God the Father, who raised him from the dead—and all those who are with me.

In part one of his greeting, Paul's main purpose is to name himself as the authors of this epistle. As you read these verses, what words help contribute to that main point, and what words look like side notes? If we take away what appears to be a side-note, marked by dashes in the translation above, we are left with Paul's main point that he and those who are with him are the authors of Galatians:

> "Paul, an apostle, and all those who are with me."

What about the side note? What is it trying to communicate?

> "—sent not by a group of people, nor by any individual person, but by Jesus Christ and God the Father, who raised him from the dead—"

The side note is placed there by Paul as a way of planting into his reader's minds the notion that his authority as an Apostle is to be trusted. He wasn't sent as an Apostle by other humans; he was sent directly by Jesus.[1] This will become more explicit as the letter continues, but for now it appears that Paul wants his readers to recognize from the beginning of the epistle that as a true Apostle, he can be trusted.

## The Formal Greeting

Paul greets each of his audiences throughout his New Testament epistles with the words "grace and peace." Of all that could be said about these words, I find it most interesting that by using them Paul is combining typical greetings of the two cultures that comprised the early Church. Grace (*charis*) is Paul's play on the formal Greek greeting of *chairein*, while his use of Peace is a nod to the traditional Hebrew greeting of *shalom*. As in the rest of his letters, Paul greets the Galatians with both Greek and Hebrew concepts in mind. This is an especially fitting greeting in a letter that addresses the relationship between Gentiles (commonly called Greeks) and the Hebrew Law.

### The Rebuke 1:6–9

The occasion and purpose of Galatians becomes clear by the sixth verse: Paul is upset with the Galatian Christians for believing the gospel of the Teachers. Our first glimpse of Paul's strong language is found in this rebuke. He takes issue with the Galatian Christians as well as the Teachers who are misleading them. According to Paul, the Galatians are not just dabbling in a different theological system by listening to the Teachers, they are deserting God, and abandoning the only true Gospel (1:6). Paul does not simply disagree with the Teachers and their approach to Christianity, he

---

1. The word apostle literally means "one who is sent", a notion that Paul is bringing to mind in this side note.

accuses them of "perverting the gospel of Christ." His rebuke ends with what could be described as exacerbated hyperbole: "If anyone — including myself! — preaches to you a gospel that is contrary to the one I already preached to you, may they go to hell (1:8–9)!" At this point in the letter, Paul certainly has the attention of his readers.

## Paul's Personal Plea: You can trust me (1:10—2:14)

After his rebuke, Paul lays out several reasons why the Gospel that he preached is to be trusted over against the gospel presented by the Teachers. As we take a look at some of the features of this plea, keep in mind that Cephas is another name for the Apostle Peter.

Throughout this section, Paul uses his own conversion as a way of earning trust among the Galatians. If Paul wanted to seek the favor of men, he would have never left his respectable life among the Pharisees in order to become a slave of Christ (1:10, 13–16).

In an allusion to his conversion on the road to Damascus, he reminds the Galatians that he didn't receive the gospel from another person, but directly from Jesus himself (1:11–12).

While Paul insists that the gospel he preached to the Galatians was revealed to him directly from God, he made it a point to emphasize that it was also in line with the gospel being preached by the rest of the Apostles.

In 1:16—2:10 Paul sketches a roughly seventeen year history of his early interaction with the other Apostles following his conversion. Paul was converted through a direct revelation of Jesus on the road to Damascus, received the gospel, and immediately retreated by himself into Arabia. After three years, he personally visited Peter and James in Jerusalem, only to leave again in order to begin planting churches throughout Syria and Cilicia. Fourteen years later, he returned to Jerusalem to make sure that the Gospel he had been preaching among the Gentiles was the same as the gospel the other Apostles were preaching among the Jews. This meeting resulted in the explicit approval of Paul's message by

James, Peter, and John, the "pillars" of the church. If his primary goal throughout this section of the epistle is to convince his readers that the Gospel he preached is in line with the Gospel being preached by the other Apostles, he has done a great job so far.

The first time I studied Galatians I remember thinking to myself that Paul should have ended this portion of his epistle here. I thought this because, at first glance, Galatians 2:11–14 is a curious anecdote for Paul to include in his epistle.

> But when Cephas came to Antioch, I opposed him to his face, because he had clearly done wrong. Until certain people came from James, he had been eating with the Gentiles. But when they arrived, he stopped doing this and separated himself because he was afraid of those who were pro-circumcision. And the rest of the Jews also joined with him in this hypocrisy, so that even Barnabas was led astray with them by their hypocrisy. But when I saw that they were not behaving consistently with the truth of the gospel, I said to Cephas in front of them all, "If you, although you are a Jew, live like a Gentile and not like a Jew, how can you try to force the Gentiles to live like Jews?"

What does Paul stand to gain by relaying the fact that he and Peter disagreed on the very issue being debated throughout Galatians? Does this not diminish the credibility he just gained by sharing the approval he received from the other Apostles in Jerusalem?

In sharing this information with the Galatians, Paul is not just being transparent, he is also making a powerful point. It appears that the same issue faced in Galatia had already been faced elsewhere in the church. Paul is admitting that the question of whether or not Gentiles should be required to follow the Law has been wrestled with even among the Apostles. In his transparency, however, he is not allowing room for the Galatians to continue believing what the Teachers are presenting. This may have been a difficult question within the church, but that does not mean that there are two equally compelling answers. In recalling his confrontation with Peter, Paul is setting himself up as the authoritative

Apostle on the matter. If he can rebuke and correct Peter on this issue, he can rebuke and correct the Galatians and their Teachers.[2]

## Summary of Galatians 1:1—2:14

Paul greets the churches in Galatia as an authoritative Apostle, rebukes them for turning away from the Gospel he originally preached to them, and convinces them that he is to be trusted more than the Teachers who have moved in to Galatia in his absence.

## This Time Through Galatians

As you make your way through Galatians this time, make note of every time Paul references his previous life. What aspects of his previous life as a Pharisee does he incorporate into his argument? Why do you think he includes this information?

---

2. Most modern English Bible translations agree that Paul's words to Peter are found in 2:14, and that 2:15 and beyond represent a return to Paul addressing the Galatians directly. Some interpreters throughout history have proposed that some of what is found in the next section of Galatians, specifically 2:15–16, is actually a continuation of the words Paul shared with Peter. There is some merit to this idea, and I think it may help make sense of some of Paul's choice of words in 2:15–16, but it does not affect our understanding of the message of Galatians in any significant way. In this book I have chosen to follow the opinion of most modern English translations by treating 2:15 and beyond as the beginning of a new section.

# 6

# Paul's Theological Argument, Part 1: Galatians 2:15—3:29

NOW THAT PAUL HAS greeted the Galatians, rebuked them for turning away from the one true Gospel, and convinced them that he can be trusted more than the Teachers, he moves on to a compelling theological argument in defense of the Gospel that he originally preached to them.

In 2:15—3:29, Paul will lay out the major premise of his argument (2:15–21), and then give four theological arguments in favor of his premise (3:1–29).[1]

## The Premise of Paul's Theological Argument: 2:15–21

J. Louis Martyn paints a compelling picture of Paul's attitude in 2:14–16. After having rebuked Peter rather harshly in 2:14, Paul "rhetorically puts his arm around Peter" in 2:15–16.

> We are Jews by birth and not Gentile sinners, yet we know that no one is justified by the works of the law but by the faithfulness of Jesus Christ. And we have come to believe in Christ Jesus, so that we may be justified by the faithfulness of Christ and not by the works of the law, because by the works of the law no one will be justified.

1. While I am sure that others have expressed it similarly, I have found the work of the late Dr. David Scholer of Fuller Seminary to be helpful in organizing the arguments made throughout these chapters.

It is as though Paul is saying to Peter, "Look, brother, we were born Jews (and by virtue of that, we have an extremely high regard for the Law), and yet *even we* know that a man is not justified by the works of the Law but through the faithfulness of Jesus Christ." At this point, Paul's attention turns back from his conflict with Peter in Antioch to addressing his readers concerning the conflict in Galatia. In 2:16 Paul will give perhaps the clearest presentation of the his argument throughout Galatians. Before we get there, we need to briefly address how to best translate a key phrase found in 2:16 and beyond.

## Faith in Jesus Christ or the Faithfulness of Jesus Christ?

We find three Greek words in Galatians 2:16 that have been the subject of much debate among scholars. This phrase, versions of which are actually found twice in this verse, appears in Greek as *pistis Christou Iesou*. There are two ways of translating this phrase, both of which make sense grammatically.

The first option is translating the phrase as "faith in Christ Jesus," which places an emphasis on the human response to Christ's work on our behalf. Translated in this way, Galatians 2:16 would read "we know that a man is not justified by works of the Law but through faith in Jesus Christ." Paul's point would be that we are not made right in God's eyes by doing the works of the Old Testament Law, but by having "faith in Jesus."

The second option is translating the phrase as "the faith of Christ Jesus," or "the faithfulness of Christ Jesus," placing the emphasis not on our response to Jesus, but on Jesus and his own faithfulness to God the Father. Translated in this way, 2:16 would read "we know that a man is not justified by works of the Law but through the faithfulness of Christ Jesus." Paul's point would be that we are not made right in God's eyes because we can perform the works of the Law ourselves, but rather because of Jesus' own perfect faithfulness to God.

Both understandings of this Greek phrase represent ideas that are present throughout the New Testament. In fact, both of these understandings are found in Galatians 2:16 alone! Christians are made right with God because of the faithfulness of Christ Jesus, and we are made right with God through faith in Christ Jesus. Or, put another way: Christians are made right with God because of what Jesus accomplished for us (the faithfulness of Christ), and we are made right with God by trusting in what Jesus accomplished for us (faith in Christ). If both of these concepts are present throughout the New Testament, does it really matter how we interpret this phrase in Galatians 2:16?

Think back to what we learned in chapter 2: How to Read an Epistle. This question matters when we seek to discover what specifically Paul was trying to communicate in Galatians. Is his emphasis here on *our own* faith in Jesus, or is his emphasis on *Jesus' own* faithfulness in fulfilling the Law? It is our responsibility as readers to do what we can to understand the exact point Paul is trying to make in Galatians, regardless of other points he makes elsewhere in the New Testament.

I think that translating *pistis Christou Iesou* as "the faithfulness of Christ Jesus" is a better representation of what Paul is communicating in 2:16, which I translate as:

"We know that a person is not justified through works of the Law but rather through the faithfulness of Christ Jesus, and so now we have trusted in Christ Jesus, in order to be justified by the faithfulness of Christ and not by works of the Law, because no one will be justified by works of the Law."

Paraphrased, Paul appears to be arguing in 2:16 that:

"A person is not made right with God by doing the works of the Law, but rather by what Christ Jesus accomplished. Because of this reality, we have placed our trust in Jesus, in order to be made right by what he accomplished and not by the works of the Law, since no one can be made right by obedience to the Law."

This becomes the premise of Paul's theological argument throughout the letter: people are made righteous by God through the faithfulness of Christ, and not through the works of the Old Testament Law.[2]

---

2. It is important to remember here that Paul wrote this letter in the

## An Objection to Paul's Gospel and his response: 2:17–21

After laying out this premise in 2:16, Paul spends the next few verses anticipating a possible objection to his understanding of the Gospel, one that may have been raised directly by the Teachers. The objection to Paul's Gospel goes something like this:

> "Let's say that we are justified by what Jesus accomplished. Now that we are counted as righteous by God, how do our lives reflect that reality? What distinguishes us from Gentiles and sinners? We must continue to practice works of the Old Testament Law, otherwise we are no different from sinners. If we stop performing works of the Law just because Jesus died for us on the cross, then isn't his death on the cross just enabling us to live a life of sin?"

The Teachers object to Paul's Gospel, in part, because they think it makes Christ an agent of sin. Paul responds to this objection with the Greek equivalent of "absolutely not!"[3] Paul often uses this exact phrase throughout the New Testament when he raises potential objections to his teaching. As logical as the Teachers' argument may seem on the surface, Paul could not disagree with it more emphatically.

Paul gives a brief response to this objection in 2:18–21. He begins with a very personal argument in 2:18: if he were now to begin teaching that Christians were required to be circumcised or perform other works of the Law, he would be going against the very Gospel he had been preaching for nearly two decades. If the Teachers are correct, then the content of Paul's entire career of preaching the Gospel among Gentiles was in vain.

---

first century of the Christian Church. When he uses the phrase "works of the Law" he has in mind specifically an obedience to the Jewish Law found in the Old Testament. While Galatians can be helpful in navigating the many faith vs. works debates we have today and have had throughout the history of the Church, it is important to avoid reading those debates into the text of Galatians. We should allow Paul to address specifically those things that he intends to address.

3. *mē genoito*, literally "May it never be so!"

In 2:19-21 Paul gives a more theological response to the objection. This section is not easy to understand. Paul hints at many ideas that he will elaborate upon throughout Galatians and elsewhere in the New Testament. Each of the following points will be unpacked later in Galatians, but for now Paul presents them without further explanation. The reader is asked to run with Paul on the following premises:

1. When Jesus died, the Law died with him. (This will be explained further in Galatians 3:23-25.)

2. Paul has been united with Christ, so when Jesus died, Paul died with Him. (Paul revisits this concept in Galatians 6:14 and Romans 7:4.)

3. Therefore Paul is now dead to the Law, and alive to Christ. To continue to do the works of the Law would be to serve a dead master at the expense of a living one.

Remember that Paul is responding to a potential objection raised by the Teachers here. They claim that performing works of the Law is necessary for Christians as a way of distinguishing themselves from the rest of the world. These Teachers are claiming to believe in Jesus. They simply want all who believe in Jesus to also perform certain works of the Law, including circumcision, as a way of distinguishing themselves from the world.

Paul's response to this objection is both simple and profound. "Why do I no longer perform the works of the Law? Not because I am a proponent of violating God's Law, but because the Law itself is dead, and we have a new master."

## Paul's Theological Argument

After writing against an objection raised by the Teachers, Paul begins in 3:1 to lay out a six-part theological argument in favor of his understanding of the Gospel. In Galatians 3 Paul will present four of these arguments, followed by a brief preview of what we will find in the last section of the epistle. He will then return to his two remaining theological arguments in Galatians 4.

Each of these six theological arguments, scattered throughout Galatians 3 and 4, are smaller pieces of a larger argument in favor of Paul's understanding of the Gospel. In each of them we should expect to find further reasons to trust that the Christian life does not include a requirement for performing works of the Law.

## Argument 1: From the Galatians' own experience (3:1–5)

Paul's first argument is an appeal to the Galatians' own conversion experience. After rebuking them a second time, calling them both foolish and bewitched, Paul asks them a question: how did you initially receive the Holy Spirit? Was it by being circumcised, or was it by hearing the Gospel and responding in faith? After his readers have answered this rhetorical question—"well, I guess it was by hearing the Gospel and responding in faith"—Paul moves in with his argument: If God *gave* you the Holy Spirit by faith, then he will *sustain* you in the Spirit by faith as well. God is not going to bait-and-switch you by converting you with faith and then requiring you to perform works of the Law in order to remain converted.

> Argument 1: If you originally received the Spirit by faith, you will continue in the Spirit by faith as well.

## Argument 2: From the Old Testament Narrative (3:6–14)

This is the first of several of Paul's arguments that rely heavily upon the Old Testament. Paul quotes the Old Testament at least six times in these nine verses. The Galatian Christians were Gentiles, and before Paul came to them they would have had little interaction with the Old Testament. Why would Paul depend so heavily upon the Old Testament when writing an epistle to a group of Gentiles?

It is possible that Paul is aware that the Teachers would eventually read his epistle. Though his main purpose is to convince the Galatians to trust his gospel, he may also be arguing in a way that appeals to the Teachers themselves. This might explain his extensive use of the Old Testament; by arguing from these Hebrew Scriptures he is able to defeat the logic of the Teachers on their own grounds. But there is a bigger reason why Paul would choose to use the Old Testament in his argument, even if his audience was not entirely familiar with it: he viewed the Old Testament as *Christian* Scriptures. Any notion that Christianity is divorced from with the God of the Old Testament cannot remain after reading Galatians. From the earliest of Christian writings, we see a high view of the Old Testament among New Testament authors.

So what exactly is Paul arguing from the Old Testament in this section? Put simply, Paul is showing that even the Old Testament itself teaches that people are made right with God through faith, and not obedience to the Law. In fact, Paul makes this argument from a section of the Old Testament known as the Pentateuch or Torah, which is the Hebrew word for Law. Paul reminds his readers that Abraham was counted as righteous by faith, and that he lived his entire life before the Law was given to Israel. Paul doesn't stop there. He goes on to argue that God's promise to Abraham, given before the Law was given, actually included a promise that Gentiles would one day be included in God's family.

> Argument 2: The Old Testament itself teaches that justification is by faith, and that God's plan from the beginning was to include Gentiles in his family.

## Argument 3: A Greco-Roman legal example (3:15–18)

Paul's next argument is based on general legal practices of the Greco-Roman world. Generally speaking, these same basic principles are found in our own legal systems today.[4] Once a last will and testimony is ratified, no one can ignore or change it. Likewise,

---

4. It is not entirely clear which specific legal practices Paul had in mind. His argument depends on an example that does not allow a will to be changed once it is in place, so some have proposed a Roman *fidei commissum* or a Hebrew *mattenat bari.*

God's promises to Abraham, given centuries before the Law was given, were not changed when the Law came. If Abraham was counted righteous by faith, then the coming of the Law did not change that reality.

Paul also takes this opportunity to share with the Galatians that while Isaac, Jacob, and the rest of Abraham's descendents are important, God's promise to Abraham was actually centered around one particular descendent: Jesus Christ. This is what Paul means in 3:16 when he insists that the promises were made to Abraham's offspring (singular), not his offsprings (plural). This is not something that appears blatantly in the text of Genesis, but it does represent a Christian understanding of God's promises to Abraham. Among other things, Jesus was the promised "offspring" of Abraham mentioned throughout Genesis. Paul once again uses the Old Testament to support his understanding of the Gospel.

> Argument 3: The Law, which came centuries after God's original promises to Abraham, did not change God's original promises to Abraham.

## Argument 4: The Law has already served its purpose (3:19–26)

If Abraham was counted as righteous by his faith, and if Jesus was the intended descendent through which the promise made to Abraham would be fulfilled, then why does the Law appear between Abraham and Jesus? Why was the Law ever given?

Paul's answer to this question is as direct as the question itself: the Law was given *as a guardian* until Jesus came. Some translations use the word custodian, tutor, or legal guardian. All of these English words are attempting to capture the concept of a temporary and necessary overseer who is in charge of a person for a given time. Implicit in this analogy is the notion that the Law had a specific purpose to serve, and that its purpose has already been fulfilled now that Jesus has come.

My wife and I want our children to be amazed by the world. We want them to enter into the fullness of exploring God's creation and the people he loves dearly. We hope they travel often and meet all kinds of different people, sharing with them the love of God. This has been our wish for them since before they were even born.

Our oldest daughter turned three this year. At this point in her life, there are several necessary restrictions that we place on her freedom. The kind of restrictions that would drive us all as crazy as they drive her. She cannot go up or down stairs without holding our hand. She can't walk by herself in a parking lot. If she were to dart towards a street, I would go to extreme lengths to prevent her from getting there. I would forcefully tackle my three-year-old daughter to the ground to prevent her from walking into traffic. I completely understand how harsh this might appear to onlookers, but that does not change my convictions that it would be the right thing to do.

So do these restrictions go against our original desires for our daughter? Not at all. They are necessary, for a time. Without them it is very possible that she will never become an adult. But one day, these restrictions will no longer be in place. She will walk freely up and down stairs and in parking lots. She will be able (even encouraged) to cross streets by herself.

Once the time comes for those restrictions to be lifted, we hope that she realizes something important: while these restrictions were temporary, and while she is no longer bound to them, they were also not *contrary* to our original desires for her. The principles behind our restrictions, even though the restrictions themselves are dead, are actually very much still alive. The restriction against crossing the street without holding my hand was put into place to prevent her from being struck by a car. Once she is old enough to cross the street by herself, we will remove that restriction. But the removal of that restriction does not negate the principle behind the restriction itself: we still do not want her to be struck by a car.

The Law had a purpose, and it was a noble one: to reveal the sin of humanity, and to preserve humanity until Christ came. But this Law, Paul argues, always had an end in mind. And that end came with the life, death, resurrection, and ascension of Jesus.

Argument 4: When Jesus came, the Law's purpose was fulfilled.

## One in Christ

The final three verses of Galatians 3 do not introduce a new argument but rather serve two purposes: (1) they re-enforce Paul's existing argument, and (2) they hint at some of the practical implications of Paul's gospel that he will unpack in chapters 5 and 6 of his epistle.

In an effort to preserve God's people from many of the destructive practices of neighboring nations, the Law made certain distinctions between Jews and Gentiles, and between those things that are "clean" and those that are "unclean." While these divisions—like all divisions—were often abused, they also provided a way to distinguish God's people from the rest of the world. In the Old Testament, a Gentile would be required to be circumcised and adhere to other restrictions put in place by the Law in order to become a part of God's family. In other words, they would convert to Judaism *through means of the Law*. Conversion and the Law went hand in hand.

To anyone familiar with the Law, Paul's words in 3:27–29 are revolutionary. Now that Jesus has come, *all* who are baptized into Christ are in God's family. If you are baptized, you belong to Christ, and you are an heir of the promises made to Abraham. This is a theme of 3:27 and 3:29. Sandwiched between these two verses is one of the most quoted verses of Galatians, and for good reason.

> There is no longer Jew or Greek, there is no longer slave or free, there is no longer male and female; for all of you are one in Christ Jesus.

In Galatians 3:28 Paul gives a poetic glimpse of what a Christian community would look like if it truly embraced this idea. Any divisions based upon differences humans have among themselves cease to matter within the community of the baptized. The distinctions themselves do not automatically cease to exist. It is not as though an ethnic Jew, like Paul, becomes a Christian and then ceases to be Jewish. Rather, any grounds for superiority or inferiority based on Paul's ethnicity is erased in his baptism. Slaves who become Christians are not automatically freed—although elsewhere in the New Testament Paul appeals to a Christian slave owner to release his slave on the grounds of his Christian faith—but any superiority or inferiority based on the slave's status is erased in her baptism. The third pair is perhaps the clearest example of this: a woman who converts to Christianity does not automatically cease to be a woman, and vice-versa, but instead any notion of superiority or inferiority based upon gender is erased in baptism.

Something about Paul's presentation of the third pair of 3:28 should cause the careful reader to pause and think. Some English translations retain a tricky nuance found in the Greek text, while others do not. In Greek, the first two pairs are juxtaposed with the word "nor," while the final pair is linked with the word "and." J. Louis Martyn's own translation captures this well:

> "There is neither Jew nor Greek; there is neither slave nor free; there is no '*male and female*'; for all of you are one in Christ Jesus."[5]

Why switch from "nor" to "and" for this final pair? Several interpreters, rather than seeing this final pair as Paul's own commentary on gender roles within the church, helpfully see his use of the phrase "male and female" as an allusion to the Genesis creation account.[6] The first pair in Galatians 3:28 emphasizes the removal of divisions based on ethnicity or religious background. The second pair emphasizes the removal of divisions based on social or economic status. The final pair, in referencing Genesis 1:27, emphasizes the removal of any other division that was characteristic of old creation, of the way things were before Jesus came and brought about new creation.

---

5. Martyn, *Galatians*, 6. Emphasis mine.

6. For a brief explanation see Wright, *Paul for Everyone*, 41–43. For a more detailed explanation see Matera, *Galatians*, 142–143 and Martyn, *Galatians*, 376–377.

Paul insists that if you are baptized into Christ, you are no longer primarily defined by your ethnicity, socio-economic status, or any other characteristic of the old creation that can cause division. This does not diminish your individuality: when you become a Christian you do not cease to be you. Our ethnic diversities do not cease to exist. Our social and economic status does not change automatically. While some of *who we are* and *what we do* will change in our conversion to Christianity, we also retain much of who we were before. In other words, I am still a white, middle-class, heterosexual married male with children. But now that I have been baptized into Christ, none of these realities can remain as my central identity, and none of these realities can be used by me to gain a sense of superiority or inferiority.

Galatians 3:28 may seem like a mere side note by Paul, but it actually fits perfectly within his argument throughout Galatians 3. If you are baptized into Christ, you are in God's family. You cannot become more part of God's family through circumcision or any other work of the Law. A Gentile convert to Christianity is "as Christian" as a Jewish convert to Christianity. All who have been baptized into Christ are "one in Christ." A requirement for a Gentile to become Jewish through circumcision in order to become truly part of God's family is a requirement that no longer makes sense now that Jesus has come.

## Summary of 2:15—3:29

In these verses, Paul lays out the premise of his Gospel: people are only made right by God through what Jesus accomplished for us, and not by performing works of the Law themselves. He then lays out four theological arguments in support of his understanding of the Gospel. (1) If you originally received the Spirit by faith, you will continue in the Spirit by faith and not by doing the works of the Law. (2) The Old Testament itself teaches that justification is by faith, and that God's plan from the beginning was to include Gentiles in his family. (3) The Law, which was given centuries after God's promises to Abraham, does not change God's original promises to Abraham. And finally, (4) when Jesus came, the Law's purpose was fulfilled.

Finally, before moving on to his next theological argument, Paul gives a glimpse of the implications of his Gospel: if you are baptized into Christ, you are a full member of God's family regardless of your previous life, and are given a new primary identity as one who belongs to Christ.

## This Time Through Galatians

We have outlined four of Paul's major theological arguments in this section. Nested within these arguments are several smaller points that are worth noting. What other arguments do you see Paul making in this section?

# 7

# Paul's Theological Argument, Part 2: Galatians 4

THE LAST TWO OF Paul's six major theological arguments are found in Galatians 4. This chapter contains a personal plea from Paul sandwiched between these two theological arguments. It is important to remember that Paul did not write verse or chapter divisions into his letter. While we divide Galatians into chapters for convenience, Paul's arguments in this chapter are building upon his arguments in the previous chapter, and are best read together. Both of the arguments in Galatians 4 require the reader to have read Galatians 3 in order to fully grasp Paul's points. This is one of many reasons why you will benefit from reading all of Galatians in one sitting as often as possible.

## Argument 5: A return to the Law is a return to Slavery (4:1–11)

As we saw in Argument 4, Paul uses the image of a guardian to describe the Law. The Law's purpose was to convict and preserve God's people for a set time, until the coming of Jesus. In Argument 5, Paul continues this analogy. The basic thrust of Paul's argument is captured in two analogies. First, to return to being under the Law would be like a freed slave returning to his former master. Secondly, it would be like a minor who had come of age and received an inheritance giving up that inheritance to return to his status as a minor. As Paul has previously argued, he again insists here that the Law's purpose has already been served. He uses the absurdity of these two analogies to show that to return to the Law now that Christ has come is futile.

Two phrases deserve further attention in this section: "basic forces of the world," found in 4:3 and 4:9, and "Abba! Father!," found in 4:6.

The Greek phrase *ta stoicheia tou kosmou* is translated a few different ways by popular English translations: "basic forces of the world" (NET), "elemental spiritual forces of the world" (NIV), or "elementary principles of the world" (ESV). Each of these translations are highlighting possible aspects of this vague Greek phrase, and taken in the context of this section of Galatians they can all be understood to refer to those things that used to serve as religious masters in the lives of the Galatian Christians. The Galatians had been freed from what Frank Matera calls "the rudimentary principles of religious life apart from Christ."[1] By being united with Christ, the Christian has been freed from those things that used to rule their religious life.

The second phrase worthy of further attention is likely a more familiar one: "Abba! Father!" Paul uses this phrase to emphasize that not only is the Christian freed from slavery to the basic forces of this world, but they are also made a child of God. Paul will expand further on this concept elsewhere in the New Testament, once again using the language of "Abba! Father!" in Romans 8:15. Why might Paul be drawn to this specific phrase, and what purpose does it serve within Galatians?

Paul's use of "Abba! Father!" is possibly a reference to Jesus's own use of this phrase, found in Mark 14:36. Jesus, the Son of God, refers to God as "Abba! Father!" Paul insists that when we become children of God, we are given the Holy Spirit which allows us to also address God as "Abba! Father!"[2] But there is perhaps

---

1. Matera, *Galatians*, 150.

2. It is important to note that in Galatians 4:6 Paul presents the Holy Spirit as the one crying out "Abba! Father!" *on our behalf.* The NET and some

another reason why Paul is so fond of this phrase, especially here in Galatians.

"Abba" is a transliteration of the Aramaic word for Father. Aramaic is the dialect of Hebrew spoken by Jews in Jesus's day, including Jesus himself. Remember back to Paul's use of "Grace and Peace" in his introduction to Galatians? We saw that by using these two words Paul is combining traditional Greek and Hebrew greetings. St. Augustine notes that Paul appears to be doing the same thing with his use of "Abba! Father!" here in Galatians 4:6:

> Now we see that he has elegantly, and not without reason, put together words from two languages signifying the same thing on behalf of the whole people, which has been called from Jews and Gentiles into the unity of faith.[3]

> Argument 5: Christians, both Jews and Gentiles, have been freed from slavery to all former masters and become children of God. To return to the Law now would constitute a return to slavery.

## A Personal Plea (4:12–20)

At this point in his epistle, Paul takes a break from his theological argument in order to make a personal plea to the Galatians. We see here a return to a passionate, yet pastoral tone. He recounts how gracious the Galatians were to him during his first visit, even though his illness placed an extra burden on them. We don't know exactly what physical illness Paul is referring to in 4:13, but it may possibly have to do with failing eyesight.[4] He then asks the Galatians, rather emphatically, "What changed?" Why were they so

---

other English translations capture this well: "God sent the Spirit of his Son into our hearts, who calls 'Abba! Father!'"

3. M. J. Edwards, *Galatians, Ancient Christian Commentary on Scripture*, 57.

4. See Galatians 4:15 and 6:11 for more.

eager to receive him the first time, and care for him so well, only to abandon his Gospel as soon as a group of outside Teachers arrives?

Paul questions the motives of the Teachers, claiming that they are using the Law to exclude the Galatians from full fellowship in the Christian community. Paul ends his plea by reminding the Galatians how much he loves them and how perplexed he is by their acceptance of the arguments of the Teachers.

## Argument 6: The Allegory of Sarah and Hagar (4:21–31)

Notice that in the transition from his plea in 4:12–20 to his final argument here in 4:21–31 Paul does not lose his passionate tone. The last thing he told the Galatians was how perplexed he was by their desire to come under the Law. He opens his final argument with an exacerbated "Ok—you who so badly want to be under the Law—do you even understand the Law?" In this argument, Paul once again returns to using the Old Testament Law itself to support his understanding of the Gospel.

At this point, it is worth pausing to read the story of Sarah and Hagar found in Genesis 16 and 21. Traditional interpretations of this story view the Jewish people as descendants of Isaac (Sarah's son) and not Ishmael (Hagar's son). To them, to be in God's family is to to be a descendent of Isaac, the child of promise, and not Ishmael, the child of the slave woman. We see this mentality in Jesus' own interaction with followers of Judaism in John 8:31–59. In fact, much of Paul's argument in this section echoes Jesus' own argument there.

It is likely that the Teachers used the story of Sarah and Hagar to defend their own perceived superiority over the Galatians. Their physical ancestry linked them to the promised child, Isaac. According to the Teachers, the Galatians—who were Gentiles and therefore more closely associated with Ishmael—needed to perform works of the Law in order to become associated with Isaac, the child of the promise.

In his final theological argument, Paul turns this approach to the story Sarah and Hagar on its head. He uses this same story to arrive at the opposite conclusion: it is the Galatian Christians, not the Teachers, who are "the children of the promise like Isaac." This understanding of the story of Sarah and Hagar is by all accounts unheard of in Paul's day. How does Paul arrive at this radical conclusion?

Paul reminds his readers of his earlier argument concerning Abraham in Galatians 3:6–14: Abraham was counted as righteous by God on account of his faith, and not on account of his adherence to the Law. When read as an allegory, Hagar represents the Law, and Sarah represents God's promises to Abraham, who was counted righteous by faith. Those who are trying to cling to the Law—the Teachers in Galatia—are actually children of the slave woman, while those who cling to faith are children of the free woman.

> Argument 6: It is those who rely on faith rather than works who are true children of Abraham.

## Summary of Galatians 4

As we have seen, Paul's final two theological arguments are presented alongside a personal plea to the Galatians. He argues that Christians have been freed from all former masters, and that a return to the Law would be a return to slavery. In reading the story of Sarah and Hagar allegorically, Paul turns the argument of the Teachers on its head by insisting that all who rely on faith rather than works of the Law are the true children of Abraham.

In the middle of these arguments, Paul issues a personal pastoral plea to the Galatians. He reminds them how graciously they welcomed and served him when he first came to them, and pleads with them as his own children to return to the true Gospel he preached to them, one where faith and not obedience to the Law is the premise of membership in God's family.

## This Time Through Galatians

As you read Galatians this time, choose a way to mark two major themes of the letter: freedom and slavery. This can be as simple as a smile next to each mention of freedom and a frown next to each mention of slavery, though I am sure you can come up with a more creative system. Each time these words or themes are addressed, mark them each individually, and then skim the letter again looking for patterns. As Paul enters into his final two chapters, these two themes will play an important role.

# 8

## The Implications of the One True Gospel: Galatians 5–6

IN GALATIANS 1–4, PAUL presents his primary argument that people are made right with God through faith and not through obedience to the Law. He walks through a six-part defense of this claim in an effort to convince the Galatian Christians that his understanding of the Gospel is correct, and the Teachers' understanding is not. If you think back to the purpose of the letter, it looks as though Paul has completed his task by the end of Galatians 4. Why, then, does he write two more chapters?

Do you remember the objection raised by the Teachers in Galatians 2:17?

> But if while seeking to be justified in Christ we ourselves have also been found to be sinners, is Christ then one who encourages sin?

The Teachers claimed that if Christians ceased to perform works of the Law because Jesus died for them on the cross, then Jesus is in some way contributing to their sin. Behind this objection is the argument that obedience to the Law is the only way for Christians to distinguish themselves from the world, and is therefore necessary. It is as though the Teachers are saying: *If we don't continue to obey the Law, how will people know that we belong to God?*

The final two chapters of Galatians give us a glimpse of Paul's longer response to this question: the true Gospel not only provides a way to make people right with God, it also enables them to live a life that distinguishes them from the world.

A community that embraced Paul's teaching in Galatians 5 and 6 would be noticeably different from the world around them.

In Galatians 1–4, Paul assures the Galatians that his understanding of the Gospel is more theologically coherent than what they had been taught by the Teachers. In Galatians 5–6, he shows how his understanding of the Gospel actually produces more fruit in the lives of both individuals and communities than the Law was ever capable of doing.

Before Paul presents these practical implications of his understanding of the Gospel, he puts in a final word for his argument against the Teachers in 5:1–12.


## Paul's Last Word on the Argument (5:1–12)

Paul has already made a convincing case that once Christ came, the Law was fulfilled and ceased to serve as a master over God's people. Based on his argument throughout this section, we can imagine that there were some Galatians who, while agreeing with Paul's overall message, were still concerned that the Teachers were correct about circumcision. *Ok, I get it, we don't have to obey the entire Law. But shouldn't we at least be circumcised, like the Teachers taught us, to show that we are truly children of God?*

As you can imagine, Paul's answer once again is an emphatic, "No!"

> Listen! I, Paul, tell you that if you let yourselves be circumcised, Christ will be of no benefit to you at all!

Once again, the power of Paul's words here need to be grasped. To be circumcised in an attempt to obey the Law and join the family of God will make Christ's work on your behalf null and void. If you try to be made right with God by obeying *part* of the Law, you will be held accountable for the entire Law. If the Law is your master in any way, you are not free. And it was "for freedom that Christ has set us free."

To drive home his point, Paul presents the Galatians with two options in 5:4–5.

> You who are trying to be declared righteous by the law have been alienated from Christ; you have fallen away from grace!
>
> For through the Spirit, by faith, we wait expectantly for the hope of righteousness.

Either the Galatians can try to be made righteous through the works of the Law, or they can wait expectantly to be made righteous through the power of the Spirit and by faith. The former is a Jesus-free Gospel; the later is a Law-free Gospel. These two gospels are not, in Paul's mind, compatible with one another.

In 5:7–12, Paul turns to discussing the Teachers themselves. It is at this point that Paul's strong language returns.

In the context of a conversation about circumcision, Paul says in 5:12 that he wishes the Teachers would even "cut themselves off." Most modern English translations have rightly kept this strong language intact in their rendering of the Greek phrase used by Paul. The word *apokopsontai* is translated "emasculate themselves" by the ESV, "castrate themselves" by the NET, and "go the whole way and emasculate themselves" by the NIV. These translations help convey the strong language Paul intentionally used in order to convince the Galatians to return to the one true Gospel.

The rest of the epistle is now concerned with painting a vision of what it would look like for a community to embrace Paul's understanding of the Gospel.

## Free to be Slaves (5:13–15)

The importance of reading Galatians in its entirety is seen clearly in chapter 5. The opening verse of this chapter stresses the freedom offered by Christ:

> For freedom Christ has set us free. Stand firm, therefore,
> and do not submit again to a yoke of slavery.

It would be tempting to stop reading after this verse and assume that our modern understanding of freedom is what Paul has in mind here. When we think of freedom, we often picture a complete lack of restrictions on our actions. We can do what we want, when we want to do it. But if we keep reading Galatians, we quickly notice that this is not at all what Paul has in mind when he uses the word freedom. In 5:1, the reader is called to "never submit again to a yoke of slavery" because "Christ has set us free." And yet as we turn to 5:13, Paul uses the same words he used in 5:1 (freedom and slavery), but the reader is left with a far different picture of freedom:

> For you were called to freedom, brothers and sisters,
> but do not use your freedom as an opportunity for
> self-indulgence, but through love become slaves to one
> another.[1]

Paul is not contradicting himself here. Christ did set us free, but the type of freedom we have in Christ is not a "I do what I want when I want" type of freedom. Those who are in Christ are freed from fulfilling the requirements of the Law in order to be considered right by God. It is for this type of freedom that Christ has set us free from the Law.

But Paul insists in 5:13–15 that while we are free from the Law, we are not free to live however we want. We are set free from the Law serving as our master, but that does not mean that we no longer have any masters. Our new master is Christ Jesus, and part of what it means to live under our new master—who came not to be served but to serve—is to become slaves to those around us.

Paul tells us that in doing so—in loving our neighbors as much as we love ourselves—we are actually getting at the heart of the purpose of the Law itself. Remember that Paul has argued that the Law, while no longer our master, is also not *contrary* to

---

1. Translation mine.

the promises of God.[2] In living out the freedom we have in Christ by serving our neighbors we are actually participating in what the Law itself originally called for.

> For the whole law can be summed up in a single commandment, namely, "*You must love your neighbor as yourself.*" (Galatians 5:14)

## Spirit and Flesh (5:16–26)

Those of us who grew up attending Vacation Bible School or participating in AWANAS are plenty familiar with the fruit of the Spirit.[3] While the virtues on display in 5:22–23 are worthy of studying on their own, they are actually used by Paul for a for a specific reason: to show that those who live by the Spirit are actually noticeably different from those who do not.

If the reader of Galatians has accepted Paul's argument up to this point, they would agree that circumcision no longer serves as a marker of belonging to God's family, and that the Law no longer serves as our master. This should lead to a couple of important questions: If circumcision is no longer a visible sign of belonging to God, then what is? If the Law is no longer our master, where do we turn for moral guidance?

The answer to both of these questions, according to Paul, is the Holy Spirit. Christians are not lacking anything by no longer being under the Law, but rather they now have a new and better *Law*: the Holy Spirit. Unlike the Old Testament Law that was written on parchment and kept safe in the Temple, the Spirit lives within each Christian. It is likely that Paul has the words of the Prophet Jeremiah in mind here, written centuries before the coming of Christ:

---

2. See Gal 3:21.

3. Most of us probably have one of a number of "Fruit of the Spirit" songs in our head at this very moment.

*"The days are coming," declares the Lord,*

*when I will make a new covenant*

*with the people of Israel*

*and with the people of Judah.*

*It will not be like the covenant*

*I made with their ancestors*

*when I took them by the hand*

*to lead them out of Egypt,*

*because they broke my covenant,*

*though I was a husband to them,"*

*declares the Lord.*

*"This is the covenant I will make with the people of Israel*

*after that time," declares the Lord.*

*"I will put my law in their minds*

*and write it on their hearts.*

*I will be their God,*

*and they will be my people.*[4]

The Spirit is the fulfillment of these words of Jeremiah. Christians, who are no longer under the Law, are not left without direction from God, but rather are guided now by the very Spirit of God. Circumcision is no longer the visible marker of those who belong to God. Want to know if someone belongs to the family of God? Don't check to see if they are circumcised, but watch their lives for patterns of love, joy, peace, patience, kindness, generosity, faithfulness, gentleness, and self control.

At this point the reader of Galatians might begin to wonder how to go about this process without damaging their relationships. What are we to do when we notice a lack of the fruit of the Spirit in the lives of those in our communities? We have all known people who fulfill the role of morality police, and we ourselves know how easy it is to judge others even when we are living in blatant sin. How are we to rightly confront one another when we notice sin in

4. Jeremiah 31:31–33

our Christian neighbor's life? Must we wait until we ourselves are free from sin?

Paul does not leave the reader to address these complicated issues alone. The following section contains Paul's guidance for how to confront one another in a Christian community without "biting and devouring one another" (5:15).

## Life Together (6:1–10)

This very practical section gives us a glimpse of Paul's approach to correcting others within the body of Christ. Paul's teaching here stresses two notions that, on the surface, appear to be conflicting: (1) we are to bear one another's burdens, and (2) all must carry their own loads. Thinking about these two notions in light of the rest of Galatians will help us make more sense of why Paul commands both simultaneously.

Think back to what Paul has already said about the Christian community in Galatians 3:

> As many of you as were baptized into Christ have clothed yourselves with Christ. There is no longer Jew or Greek, there is no longer slave or free, there is no longer male and female; for all of you are one in Christ Jesus. And if you belong to Christ, then you are Abraham's offspring, heirs according to the promise.

"All of you are one in Christ Jesus." This means that your burdens *are* my burdens. In a very real sense by bearing *your* burdens I am carrying my own load. On a more practical level, Paul is also insisting that carrying our own load frees us up to serve one another. Remember Paul's words about how we are to use our freedom?

> For you were called to freedom, brothers and sisters; only do not use your freedom as an opportunity to indulge your flesh, but through love serve one another.

By being responsible with our own freedom we are freeing ourselves up to bear someone else's burden. In Galatians 6 Paul has the specific burden of sin in mind: those who are humble are free to work alongside those who have the burden of pride. Those who have extraordinary trust in God can come alongside those who are crippled with worry.

There is no room for pride in those areas of life where we carry our load well. These are all gifts from God, given through the Holy Spirit, for the benefit of the Church. In Galatians 6 Paul calls us to use these gifts to carry the other members of the body of Christ, just as others have carried us.

In doing so, we fulfill what Paul calls the *Law of Christ*.[5] The Epilogue will explore this notion further, but for now it is helpful to think of the Law of Christ as the guiding principle that governs the universe. It is, in a sense, the Law that is above all laws. By fulfilling this *Law of Christ*, we are getting at the very heart of what our new Master, Christ Jesus himself, desires for us.

## Farewell (6:11–18)

Paul has greeted the Galatians, defended his authority as an apostle, argued in favor of his understanding of the Gospel, and painted a vision of how life in Christian community should look for those who embrace the Gospel. It is now time for him to say farewell.

Paul, as did many other New Testament authors, often dictated his letters to scribes.[6] Here in Galatians we learn that Paul himself wrote this epistle with his own hand. His mention of the large letters he used might be a reference to the physical ailment he discussed in 4:13. If perhaps Paul was beginning to have trouble with his eyesight when he first visited the Galatians, it would necessitate his writing with larger letters many years later.

Before closing the epistle, Paul has one more word concerning the Teachers. Previously in Galatians he argued against their claim that circumcision was required for full membership in God's family; here he questions their motives for making such a claim in

5. Paul is the only New Testament author to use this phrase. It appears here and in 1 Corinthians 9:21.

6. See Romans 16:22–23, for example.

the first place. Paul argues that the Teachers must stand to benefit in some way by forcing Gentiles to be circumcised. The Teachers themselves don't even follow the whole Law, but must feel some sense of superiority by forcing others to do so.

Paul's final words before his closing benediction are found in 6:14–16. As is the case for most sections of Galatians, an entire book could be written on these three verses. In hopes that this will not be the only thing you read about these powerful verses, what follows is an attempt to capture some of what Paul is trying to convey here.

When Jesus Christ was crucified, the world died, and Paul died to the world. That is to say, the *old way of relating to God*, and of *attempting to earn his favor*, died. But that is not all that died. In an echo of his words in 2:20, Paul also died to the world when Jesus was crucified. Why does Paul mention the world dying *and* his dying to the world?

Imagine being captured by an enemy ship in battle. As a prisoner, you are tied to the ship to prevent escape. You are caught in a bit of a dilemma: you know that it would propel your side to victory if this enemy ship were to sink. But you also can't help but realize that if the ship were to sink, you would go down with it. Ideally, your side would somehow be able to both sink the ship and free you from its grasp. Something like this is perhaps what Paul has in mind here.

The old way of relating to God died in the life, death, resurrection, and ascension of Jesus. But that death does not stop the old world from taking us down with it. In the crucifixion, Jesus defeated the enemy ship *and* he broke the chains that bound us to it. So now nothing from that old world counts any more. All that matters is the new world ushered in by Jesus.

> For neither circumcision nor uncircumcision counts for anything; the only thing that matters is a new creation!

## Summary of Galatians 5–6

In this final section of his epistle, Paul does more than simply say farewell. Christians have been set free in Christ. This means at least two things to Paul: (1) we can never again return to the Law or any other former master, and (2) we are bound to use our freedom to serve those around us. The fruit of the Spirit, not circumcision, now serves as a visible marker of those who belong to the family of God. As a community that is bound together as one in Christ, Christians will need to confront one another when they fall into sin.

Before saying farewell, Paul accuses the Teachers of desiring to boast in their ability to force others to obey the Law. Paul insists that the only thing Christians have to boast in is the cross of Christ, and that the only thing that matters now is the New Creation brought about by Jesus. Paul offers some concluding remarks before ending his epistle with the same word that he uses at the end of each of his New Testament works: Amen.[7]

## Amen

Most letters that we read today do not end with the word "Amen." We usually reserve this word for preachers and for prayers. Even so, it has become a staple in our vocabulary, and most of the time we say it we don't think about what it actually means.

Amen simply means, "may it be so." When we close our prayers, we are saying to God "may it be so." When a preacher makes a particularly compelling point, we tell ourselves and those sitting near us "may it be so" in our lives.

The last word Paul writes to his beloved Galatians is *Amen*. *May it be so*. May the one true Gospel of freedom in Christ be

---

7. Tucked away in this final section is a word from Paul about how to take care of those who teach the Gospel: "Now the one who receives instruction in the word must share all good things with the one who teaches it." (Galatians 6:5) Unless you have stolen this book, I want to thank you for "sharing all good things" with me through your purchase.

embraced and proclaimed and lived-out in all of Galatia, come what may. Preserved through thousands of years of history, this final word from Paul to the Galatians still reaches each of us today. *May it be so* in our lives as well.

## This Time Through Galatians

I hope that you do not consider this your *last* time through Galatians. In a very real sense, we can only now begin to study this important epistle. We have not grasped a passage of Scripture until we have lived out its truth in our lives. May this time through Galatians, and every other time through Galatians, be yet another occasion for us, by God's grace, to learn what it means to fulfill the Law of Christ.

# Epilogue

In the beginning was the Logos, and the Logos was with
God, and the Logos was God.

And the Logos became flesh and dwelt among us, and we
have seen his glory, the glory as of the Father's only Son,
full of grace and truth.

(JOHN 1:1, 14)

### From Law to Logos

BEFORE THIS BOOK WAS published, if you were to Google "From
Law to Logos" you would only see two results: (1) a sermon I
preached at Church of the Incarnation with that same title, and (2)
an English translation of an Easter sermon preached in the second
century by St. Melito, the Bishop of Sardis. (Clearly I borrowed the
title from him, and not the other way around.) Why is *From Law
To Logos* a fitting title for a book about Galatians?

We never find this exact phrase in the text of Galatians, but it
does a wonderful job of succinctly capturing Paul's understanding
of the radical shift that occurred when Jesus came.

The Greek word translated as "word" throughout John 1 is
*logos*, and as far as words go it has a fairly rich history. In the Old
Testament, God's word—his *logos*—was not just how he commu-
nicated with the world, it was also how he *acted* within the world.
Think back to the Genesis creation narrative: God *said* let there be

light, and there was light. Judaism in and around Jesus' time began to personify this *logos*, giving it names like "Wisdom." To them, the *logos* was many things: it was God's model for the universe, it was God's power within the universe, and it served as a link between God and humanity.

With all of this in mind, we now see that St. John made an astonishing claim in the prologue to his Gospel: the wisdom that created the universe—the source of all truth and physics and life and light and love—became an actual human being. The *logos* entered into the womb of a young virgin named Mary, gestated for nine months, and was born. Not sweet-movie-scene born, but dirty, dark, cold-floor-of-a-barn born. When the wisdom that created the universe enters into that very universe as a human being, something big is happening in the world.

As much as there is continuity between the Old Covenant and the New Covenant, St. Paul's epistle to the Galatians only makes sense when we realize that a fundamental shift occurred when Jesus came.

Two thousand years ago, in the suburbs of Jerusalem, God's relationship with humanity transitioned from one marked by bondage to the Law to one marked by bondage to the life-giving *Logos*.

But it is not as if the Law came first, and then was later replaced by a brand new *Logos*. Think back to John 1. The *Logos* was "there in the beginning with God" all along. God created the world, and He created *how the world should work*. The Law was given as a temporary guardian until the wisdom that created the world actually entered into that very world in the person of Jesus.

The Law was a shadow of the wisdom of God, while Jesus is the "image" of that very wisdom.[1] We can learn a lot about someone from their shadow, but no one would choose to continue to gaze upon the shadow of a person if that very person was standing right in front of them.

---

1. Paul quotes an early Christian hymn in Colossians 1:15–20. In this hymn Jesus is referred to as the "image of the invisible God."

Throughout Galatians, Paul is dealing with people who have been convinced to return to the shadow even while the flesh-and-blood person of Jesus is standing before them. In other words, he is dealing with people like you and me.

# The New English Translation of Galatians

1:1 From Paul, an apostle (not from men, nor by human agency, but by Jesus Christ and God the Father who raised him from the dead) 2 and all the brothers with me, to the churches of Galatia. 3 Grace and peace to you from God the Father and our Lord Jesus Christ, 4 who gave himself for our sins to rescue us from this present evil age according to the will of our God and Father, 5 to whom be glory forever and ever! Amen.

6 I am astonished that you are so quickly deserting the one who called you by the grace of Christ and are following a different gospel– 7 not that there really is another gospel, but there are some who are disturbing you and wanting to distort the gospel of Christ. 8 But even if we (or an angel from heaven) should preach a gospel contrary to the one we preached to you, let him be condemned to hell! 9 As we have said before, and now I say again, if any one is preaching to you a gospel contrary to what you received, let him be condemned to hell! 10 Am I now trying to gain the approval of people, or of God? Or am I trying to please people? If I were still trying to please people, I would not be a slave of Christ!

11 Now I want you to know, brothers and sisters, that the gospel I preached is not of human origin. 12 For I did not receive it or learn it from any human source; instead I received it by a revelation of Jesus Christ.

13 For you have heard of my former way of life in Judaism, how I was savagely persecuting the church of God and trying to destroy it. 14 I was advancing in Judaism beyond many of my contemporaries in my nation, and was extremely zealous for the traditions of my ancestors. 15 But when the one who set me apart from birth and called me by his grace was pleased 16 to reveal his Son in me so that I could preach him among the Gentiles, I did not go to ask advice from any human being, 17 nor did I go up to Jerusalem to see those who were apostles before me, but right away I departed to Arabia, and then returned to Damascus.

18 Then after three years I went up to Jerusalem to visit Cephas and get information from him, and I stayed with him fifteen days. 19 But I saw none of the other apostles except James the Lord's brother. 20 I assure you that, before God, I am not lying about what I am writing to you! 21 Afterward I went to the regions of Syria and Cilicia. 22 But I was personally unknown to the churches of Judea that are in Christ. 23 They were only hearing, "The one who once persecuted us is now proclaiming the good news of the faith he once tried to destroy." 24 So they glorified God because of me.

2:1 Then after fourteen years I went up to Jerusalem again with Barnabas, taking Titus along too. 2 I went there because of a revelation and presented to them the gospel that I preach among the Gentiles. But I did so only in a private meeting with the influential people, to make sure that I was not running—or had not run–in vain. 3 Yet not even Titus, who was with me, was compelled to be circumcised, although he was a Greek. 4 Now this matter arose because of the false brothers with false pretenses who slipped in unnoticed to spy on our freedom that we have in Christ Jesus, to make us slaves. 5 But we did not surrender to them even for a moment, in order that the truth of the gospel would remain with you.

6 But from those who were influential (whatever they were makes no difference to me; God shows no favoritism between people)– those influential leaders added nothing to my message. 7 On the

contrary, when they saw that I was entrusted with the gospel to the uncircumcised just as Peter was to the circumcised 8 (for he who empowered Peter for his apostleship to the circumcised also empowered me for my apostleship to the Gentiles) 9 and when James, Cephas, and John, who had a reputation as pillars, recognized the grace that had been given to me, they gave to Barnabas and me the right hand of fellowship, agreeing that we would go to the Gentiles and they to the circumcised. 10 They requested only that we remember the poor, the very thing I also was eager to do.

11 But when Cephas came to Antioch, I opposed him to his face, because he had clearly done wrong. 12 Until certain people came from James, he had been eating with the Gentiles. But when they arrived, he stopped doing this and separated himself because he was afraid of those who were pro-circumcision. 13 And the rest of the Jews also joined with him in this hypocrisy, so that even Barnabas was led astray with them by their hypocrisy. 14 But when I saw that they were not behaving consistently with the truth of the gospel, I said to Cephas in front of them all, "If you, although you are a Jew, live like a Gentile and not like a Jew, how can you try to force the Gentiles to live like Jews?"

15 We are Jews by birth and not Gentile sinners, 16 yet we know that no one is justified by the works of the law but by the faithfulness of Jesus Christ. And we have come to believe in Christ Jesus, so that we may be justified by the faithfulness of Christ and not by the works of the law, because by the works of the law no one will be justified. 17 But if while seeking to be justified in Christ we ourselves have also been found to be sinners, is Christ then one who encourages sin? Absolutely not! 18 But if I build up again those things I once destroyed, I demonstrate that I am one who breaks God's law. 19 For through the law I died to the law so that I may live to God. 20 I have been crucified with Christ, and it is no longer I who live, but Christ lives in me. So the life I now live in the body, I live because of the faithfulness of the Son of God, who loved me and gave himself for me. 21 I do not set aside God's

grace, because if righteousness could come through the law, then Christ died for nothing!

3:1 You foolish Galatians! Who has cast a spell on you? Before your eyes Jesus Christ was vividly portrayed as crucified! 2 The only thing I want to learn from you is this: Did you receive the Spirit by doing the works of the law or by believing what you heard? 3 Are you so foolish? Although you began with the Spirit, are you now trying to finish by human effort? 4 Have you suffered so many things for nothing?–if indeed it was for nothing. 5 Does God then give you the Spirit and work miracles among you by your doing the works of the law or by your believing what you heard?

6 Just as Abraham believed God, and it was credited to him as righteousness, 7 so then, understand that those who believe are the sons of Abraham. 8 And the scripture, foreseeing that God would justify the Gentiles by faith, proclaimed the gospel to Abraham ahead of time, saying, "All the nations will be blessed in you." 9 So then those who believe are blessed along with Abraham the believer. 10 For all who rely on doing the works of the law are under a curse, because it is written, "Cursed is everyone who does not keep on doing everything written in the book of the law." 11 Now it is clear no one is justified before God by the law, because the righteous one will live by faith. 12 But the law is not based on faith, but the one who does the works of the law will live by them. 13 Christ redeemed us from the curse of the law by becoming a curse for us (because it is written, "Cursed is everyone who hangs on a tree") 14 in order that in Christ Jesus the blessing of Abraham would come to the Gentiles, so that we could receive the promise of the Spirit by faith.

15 Brothers and sisters, I offer an example from everyday life: When a covenant has been ratified, even though it is only a human contract, no one can set it aside or add anything to it. 16 Now the promises were spoken to Abraham and to his descendant. Scripture does not say, "and to the descendants," referring to many, but "and to your descendant," referring to one, who is Christ. 17 What

I am saying is this: The law that came four hundred thirty years later does not cancel a covenant previously ratified by God, so as to invalidate the promise. 18 For if the inheritance is based on the law, it is no longer based on the promise, but God graciously gave it to Abraham through the promise.

19 Why then was the law given? It was added because of transgressions, until the arrival of the descendant to whom the promise had been made. It was administered through angels by an intermediary. 20 Now an intermediary is not for one party alone, but God is one. 21 Is the law therefore opposed to the promises of God? Absolutely not! For if a law had been given that was able to give life, then righteousness would certainly have come by the law. 22 But the scripture imprisoned everything and everyone under sin so that the promise could be given—because of the faithfulness of Jesus Christ—to those who believe.

23 Now before faith came we were held in custody under the law, being kept as prisoners until the coming faith would be revealed. 24 Thus the law had become our guardian until Christ, so that we could be declared righteous by faith. 25 But now that faith has come, we are no longer under a guardian. 26 For in Christ Jesus you are all sons of God through faith. 27 For all of you who were baptized into Christ have clothed yourselves with Christ. 28 There is neither Jew nor Greek, there is neither slave nor free, there is neither male nor female–for all of you are one in Christ Jesus. 29 And if you belong to Christ, then you are Abraham's descendants, heirs according to the promise.

4:1 Now I mean that the heir, as long as he is a minor, is no different from a slave, though he is the owner of everything. 2 But he is under guardians and managers until the date set by his father. 3 So also we, when we were minors, were enslaved under the basic forces of the world. 4 But when the appropriate time had come, God sent out his Son, born of a woman, born under the law, 5 to redeem those who were under the law, so that we may be adopted as sons with full rights. 6 And because you are sons, God sent the Spirit of his Son into our hearts, who calls "Abba! Father!" 7 So you are no longer a slave but a son, and if you are a son, then you are also an heir through God.

8 Formerly when you did not know God, you were enslaved to beings that by nature are not gods at all. 9 But now that you have come to know God (or rather to be known by God), how can you turn back again to the weak and worthless basic forces? Do you want to be enslaved to them all over again? 10 You are observing religious days and months and seasons and years. 11 I fear for you that my work for you may have been in vain. 12 I beg you, brothers and sisters, become like me, because I have become like you. You have done me no wrong!

13 But you know it was because of a physical illness that I first proclaimed the gospel to you, 14 and though my physical condition put you to the test, you did not despise or reject me. Instead, you welcomed me as though I were an angel of God, as though I were Christ Jesus himself! 15 Where then is your sense of happiness now? For I testify about you that if it were possible, you would have pulled out your eyes and given them to me! 16 So then, have I become your enemy by telling you the truth?

17 They court you eagerly, but for no good purpose; they want to exclude you, so that you would seek them eagerly. 18 However, it is good to be sought eagerly for a good purpose at all times, and not only when I am present with you. 19 My children—I am again undergoing birth pains until Christ is formed in you! 20 I wish I could be with you now and change my tone of voice, because I am perplexed about you.

21 Tell me, you who want to be under the law, do you not understand the law? 22 For it is written that Abraham had two sons, one by the slave woman and the other by the free woman. 23 But one, the son by the slave woman, was born by natural descent, while the

other, the son by the free woman, was born through the promise. 24 These things may be treated as an allegory, for these women represent two covenants. One is from Mount Sinai bearing children for slavery; this is Hagar. 25 Now Hagar represents Mount Sinai in Arabia and corresponds to the present Jerusalem, for she is in slavery with her children. 26 But the Jerusalem above is free, and she is our mother. 27 For it is written:

> "Rejoice, O barren woman who does not bear children;
> break forth and shout, you who have no birth pains,
> because the children of the desolate woman are more numerous
> than those of the woman who has a husband."

28 But you, brothers and sisters, are children of the promise like Isaac. 29 But just as at that time the one born by natural descent persecuted the one born according to the Spirit, so it is now. 30 But what does the scripture say? "Throw out the slave woman and her son, for the son of the slave woman will not share the inheritance with the son" of the free woman. 31 Therefore, brothers and sisters, we are not children of the slave woman but of the free woman.

5:1 For freedom Christ has set us free. Stand firm, then, and do not be subject again to the yoke of slavery. 2 Listen! I, Paul, tell you that if you let yourselves be circumcised, Christ will be of no benefit to you at all! 3 And I testify again to every man who lets himself be circumcised that he is obligated to obey the whole law. 4 You who are trying to be declared righteous by the law have been alienated from Christ; you have fallen away from grace! 5 For through the Spirit, by faith, we wait expectantly for the hope of righteousness. 6 For in Christ Jesus neither circumcision nor uncircumcision carries any weight—the only thing that matters is faith working through love.

7 You were running well; who prevented you from obeying the truth? 8 This persuasion does not come from the one who calls you! 9 A little yeast makes the whole batch of dough rise! 10 I am confident in the Lord that you will accept no other view. But the

one who is confusing you will pay the penalty, whoever he may be. 11 Now, brothers and sisters, if I am still preaching circumcision, why am I still being persecuted? In that case the offense of the cross has been removed. 12 I wish those agitators would go so far as to castrate themselves!

13 For you were called to freedom, brothers and sisters; only do not use your freedom as an opportunity to indulge your flesh, but through love serve one another. 14 For the whole law can be summed up in a single commandment, namely, "You must love your neighbor as yourself." 15 However, if you continually bite and devour one another, beware that you are not consumed by one another. 16 But I say, live by the Spirit and you will not carry out the desires of the flesh. 17 For the flesh has desires that are opposed to the Spirit, and the Spirit has desires that are opposed to the flesh, for these are in opposition to each other, so that you cannot do what you want. 18 But if you are led by the Spirit, you are not under the law. 19 Now the works of the flesh are obvious: sexual immorality, impurity, depravity, 20 idolatry, sorcery, hostilities, strife, jealousy, outbursts of anger, selfish rivalries, dissensions, factions, 21 envying, murder, drunkenness, carousing, and similar things. I am warning you, as I had warned you before: Those who practice such things will not inherit the kingdom of God!

22 But the fruit of the Spirit is love, joy, peace, patience, kindness, goodness, faithfulness, 23 gentleness, and self-control. Against such things there is no law. 24 Now those who belong to Christ have crucified the flesh with its passions and desires. 25 If we live by the Spirit, let us also behave in accordance with the Spirit. 26 Let us not become conceited, provoking one another, being jealous of one another.

6:1 Brothers and sisters, if a person is discovered in some sin, you who are spiritual restore such a person in a spirit of gentleness. Pay close attention to yourselves, so that you are not tempted too. 2 Carry one another's burdens, and in this way you will fulfill the law of Christ. 3 For if anyone thinks he is something when he is nothing, he deceives himself. 4 Let each one examine his own work. Then he can take pride in himself and not compare himself with someone else. 5 For each one will carry his own load.

6 Now the one who receives instruction in the word must share all good things with the one who teaches it. 7 Do not be deceived. God will not be made a fool. For a person will reap what he sows, 8 because the person who sows to his own flesh will reap corruption from the flesh, but the one who sows to the Spirit will reap eternal life from the Spirit. 9 So we must not grow weary in doing good, for in due time we will reap, if we do not give up. 10 So then, whenever we have an opportunity, let us do good to all people, and especially to those who belong to the family of faith.

11 See what big letters I make as I write to you with my own hand!

12 Those who want to make a good showing in external matters are trying to force you to be circumcised. They do so only to avoid being persecuted for the cross of Christ. 13 For those who are circumcised do not obey the law themselves, but they want you to be circumcised so that they can boast about your flesh. 14 But may I never boast except in the cross of our Lord Jesus Christ, through which the world has been crucified to me, and I to the world. 15 For neither circumcision nor uncircumcision counts for anything; the only thing that matters is a new creation! 16 And all who will behave in accordance with this rule, peace and mercy be on them, and on the Israel of God.

17 From now on let no one cause me trouble, for I bear the marks of Jesus on my body.

18 The grace of our Lord Jesus Christ be with your spirit, brothers and sisters. Amen.

# Bibliography

Edwards, M. J., ed. *Galatians, Ephesians, Philippians*. Ancient Christian Commentary on Scripture. Downers Grove, IL: InterVarsity, 1999.

Martyn, J. Louis. *Galatians: A New Translation with Introduction and Commentary*. Vol. 33A. Anchor Yale Bible. London: Yale University Press, 2008.

Matera, Frank J. *Galatians*. Edited by Daniel J. Harrington. Vol. 9. Sacra Pagina Series. Collegeville, MN: The Liturgical Press, 2007.

Wright, Tom. *Paul for Everyone: Galatians and Thessalonians*. London: Society for Promoting Christian Knowledge, 2004.

Made in the USA
San Bernardino, CA
09 June 2019